A LETTER TO MY READERS

Dear Friends,

I love to read good, strong stories with lots of adventure, action, and emotion—and plenty of detail. No surprise it's the kind of story I like to write, too.

That's what this series, I Witness, is all about: exciting stories about fictional young people during real events in history. I Witness stories will make you feel as if you are right in the middle of the action. The illustrations will show what things really looked like.

There have been many gold rushes in American history, but since I live in Colorado, the one I've heard most about is the gold rush of 1859—the days of "Pike's Peak or Bust." Hard Gold is as true to what happened to those Fifty-Niners as I could make it. I don't know if there actually was a teenager by the name of Early Wittcomb, but I am sure there were a good many like him.

Here we go . . .

AVI

AN I WITNESS NOVEL

HARD GOLD

THE
COLORADO GOLD RUSH
OF 1859

A TALE OF
THE OLD WEST

Disney • HYPERION BOOKS
NEW YORK

Text copyright © 2008 by Avi

All rights reserved. Published by Disney • Hyperion Books, an imprint of Disney Book Group. No part of this book may be reproduced or transmitted in any form or by any means, electronic or mechanical, including photocopying, recording, or by any information storage and retrieval system, without written permission from the publisher.

For information address Disney • Hyperion Books,
114 Fifth Avenue, New York, New York 10011-5690.

First Disney • Hyperion paperback edition, 2009
10 9 8 7 6 5 4 3 2 1
Printed in the United States of America
Library of Congress Cataloging-in-Publication Data on file.
ISBN: 978-1-4231-0520-6
Visit www.hyperionbooksforchildren.com
Illustration credits appear on page 230.
ILS No. J689-1817-1
110 2009

For Bev Robin and Leslie Blauman

CONTENTS

CHAPTER ONE

How It Began

Late Winter, 1858

MY NAME is Early Wittcomb, and I'm the teller of this tale. I was given the name *Early* because I was born in the first hour of the first day of 1845—the same year the Republic of Texas joined the Union. While I can't say I was *always* early, I did stay—otherwise I wouldn't be telling this story, now would I?

This tale really begins when "Old Buck" James Buchanan was president, the one just before Lincoln. That was about the time that a drought had settled on the whole middle part of the country, including Iowa state, where my family had a farm.

Our seventy-five acres were in Cass County, east of

Just a glimpse of how the prairie looked.
To my eyes it wasn't nearly so cultivated, not back in 1858.

the town of Wiota. We grew wheat, corn, and oats and
kept some sheep, hogs, and cows.

Having less rain meant we weren't able to grow much,
so money was scarce. Markets were so bad they were calling it a "panic." Even if you had money, it was hard to
keep. Lots of farm folks couldn't make mortgage payments
to the bank. If you couldn't pay, the bank took the farm.
Called "foreclosure." Perfectly legal, in a kind of low-
down, thieving, rascally way.

Pa and Ma used savings to pay our mortgage, but with
no cash coming in, our money was dwindling. We didn't
know what might happen.

Then, on a cold morning in February, a gig pulled by a glossy brown mare drove up to our house. That didn't happen often, so the whole family—Pa, Ma, Adam, Uncle Jesse, and I—went out to see who it was.

At the reins of the gig was Mr. Fuslin, our local banker. Fuslin was not only head of the local Whig party but a county judge. A portly man, he had a gray beard that edged round his long face like an upside-down crown. Hatchet-nosed.

Sitting next to him was a tall, skinny fellow dressed in top hat, a long black frock coat, black vest, and fine boots. Never saw him before. They both climbed out.

A gig, such as Judge Fuslin had. Pretty fancy and expensive. Most folks around Wiota used wagons to get around.

The judge tipped his top hat to Ma, and nodded toward Adam, my older brother. He ignored Uncle Jesse and me. Then, to my Pa, he says, "Mr. Wittcomb, it's my pleasure to introduce you to my friend"—meaning the fellow next to him—"Mr. Zebulon Bigalow."

"Obliged, sir," Pa said.

"Mr. Wittcomb, sir," Mr. Bigalow proclaimed, "I represent the great Chicago and North Western Railway."

The way he spread those words through the air, you could tell he expected us to bow down, put lips to earth, and cry "Hallelujah!"

"Yes, sir," said Pa. "What can I do for you?" Being polite was our way.

"You'll be glad to know," said this Bigalow fellow, "that after careful surveying, our railroad requires your farmland for a right-of-way. It would be good for Cass County. Good for Iowa. Good for the whole United States of America. And very good for you, sir."

"Is that so?"

"Yes, sir. I've been authorized to give you two thousand dollars for an outright purchase of your land. What's more, we'll take over all mortgage debts."

Knowing that was a whole pile of money, I looked to Pa to see his reaction. He was stony-faced.

The judge jumped in. "Daniel, may I be bold enough to advise that this is a good offer. A fine offer. You should take it up."

Next moment, Mr. Bigalow reached into his carpetbag and plumped out a bulging fist of cash. Held it toward Pa.

A rare thing, but Pa turned hot. I even saw the tips of his ears get red. "No thank you, sir," he said, a touch of tremble in his voice. "This farm is going to be left to my boy." He meant Adam.

"You surprise me, sir," said Mr. Bigalow. "This is a generous offer. I'm not a threatening man, but if you refuse, the Chicago and North Western Railway might well have to find a way to make you sell the land to them."

"They do have strength, Mr. Wittcomb," put in Judge Fuslin. "And you do have debts."

That being a threat if I ever heard one, I started getting mad. I glanced at my brother Adam. He was red-faced, fuming, clenching fists. But he didn't do anything.

But my uncle Jesse, he stepped forward and said, "Gentlemen, you heard what Mr. Wittcomb said. We'd be more than obliged if you'd leave. But if you don't know how, I'd be happy to get my Sharps slant rifle and teach you."

"Young man, do you know whom you're threatening?" demanded Judge Fuslin.

"I sure do," said Jesse. He was putting on some serious frowning, but I could tell by his bright eyes that he was enjoying himself.

"Jesse!" said Pa, but he didn't say more.

I can tell you, I grinned when those fellows leaped into their gig and clattered off.

As we returned to the house, Adam said, "Jesse, you're a fool to threaten those people."

"You're a fool not to," Jesse threw back. Those two were always sparring.

"I'm just glad they went away," said Ma.

Pa, as usual, didn't say more than he already had.

Later on, Jesse and I talked about what had happened. Considering the railway man's warning, I was pretty upset.

"Early," he said, "don't worry. It's just Judge Fuslin on the hustle, wanting everything his own way. Nothing's going to happen."

But the truth is, because of Pa's refusing to sell the farm—everything did change.

CHAPTER TWO

My Brothers

NOW, HERE'S what you have to know about my two brothers.

Brother Adam, nine years older than me, was a strong, stocky fellow with a set of chin whiskers, of which he was proud. Worked hard, I'll give him that; but he liked being in charge. The truth was, my folks were getting weary, with gray hair and as many lines on their faces as furrows in our fields. Toiling dawn to dusk in dust had left them worn and fretful. They weren't just willing to let Adam run things—we all knew that some day he was going to inherit the farm.

"Don't forget I'm your older brother," Adam liked

to say when telling me what to do, which he did pretty regular. Or if I fussed, he'd actually say, "Look here, Early, when the time comes, the farm will be mine, not yours." Didn't like him saying it, but I had no choice. I just worked.

Now, Jesse—he was completely different. Most folks hear the word "uncle" and you think, an *older* fellow. Truth is, though Jesse truly was my uncle—my ma's brother—he was just nineteen years old, a whole lot younger than Ma and only six years older than me.

See, soon after Jesse was born, he became an orphan. Ma raised him up by hand, so to speak. While Jesse had a different last name than me, he was my real brother as far back as I could remember. In fact, he called me "little brother."

Five feet eight inches tall, he had wild golden hair and an ambling, shambling walk I could have picked out in a crowd of a million. He had a *golly, good morning!* smile that made me glad he was around, especially since my family wasn't given much to smiling. Clean shaven, too. "Who wants to look like a goat?" he'd say, winking at Adam, who sported that dangling beard.

Adam envied Jesse. Jesse had real good hands, hands that could split a rail in three whacks, shoot a flying pigeon at fifty yards, or turn a willow stick into a whistle in the time it took a fellow to spell Mississippi. Wasn't it Jesse who taught me how to ride, fish, and shoot his own slant-breach Sharps rifle? We bunked in the same room, too, and great glory, how he made me laugh with his jokes and stories! I have to admit I worshipped Jesse like he was a hero made of gold.

And the thing is, it's *gold* that this story is all about.

CHAPTER THREE

Bad News and Good

September 1858

LIKE I said, my folks were paying our mortgage with their savings. Thing was, those savings were going fast, because the drought hadn't eased. So Pa and Adam hitched the mule to our buggy and clattered to town to meet with our banker to make some kind of arrangement. Who was that banker? None other than that Judge Fuslin I already told you about. Jesse went along for the ride.

They came back with bad news. Judge Fuslin was not going to budge: unless the mortgage was paid, we were going to lose our farm. The only positive thing was that the folks had about twelve months of money left in their savings.

That night we sat around the kitchen table staring with sad eyes at the whale-oil lamp, burning low like a last hope. There didn't seem to be much doubt about what was going to happen. I never saw my parents so discouraged. After all their toilsome work, too.

Well, anyway, we were sitting there silent as snow, not knowing what to do, when Jesse pulled out a newspaper— the Kansas City *Journal of Commerce*—which he'd found in town. "Look here," he said with that cheerful grin of his, "we should consider this." He held up the paper so we could read the headlines:

The New Eldorado!

GOLD IN KANSAS TERRITORY!

The Pike's Peak Mines!

The First Arrival of Gold Dust in Kansas City!

He went on to read the story under the headlines:

"We were surprised this morning to meet Monsieur Bordeau and company, old mountain traders just in from Pike's Peak in the Kansas Territory. They came in for outfits, tools, etc., for working the newly discovered mines on Cherry Creek, a tributary of the South Platte. They brought several ounces of gold, dug up by the trappers of that region, which, in fairness, equals the choicest of California specimens.

"Mr. John Cantrell, an old citizen of Westport, has three ounces which he dug with a hatchet in Cherry Creek and washed out with a frying pan. Monsieur Richard, an old French trapper, has several ounces of the precious dust which he dug with an ax.

"Kansas City is alive with excitement, and parties are already preparing for the diggings!"

Soon as Jesse read that I knew exactly what was on his mind: this Kansas gold might be something we needed to find out about. After all, the Kansas Territory was just southwest of our own Iowa state. My parents, though, they looked at Jesse as if he'd just announced he was placing a five-dollar bet on a three-legged ox in a six-mile horse race.

Adam said, "I don't believe it."

"Read it yourself," said Jesse, flipping the paper down.

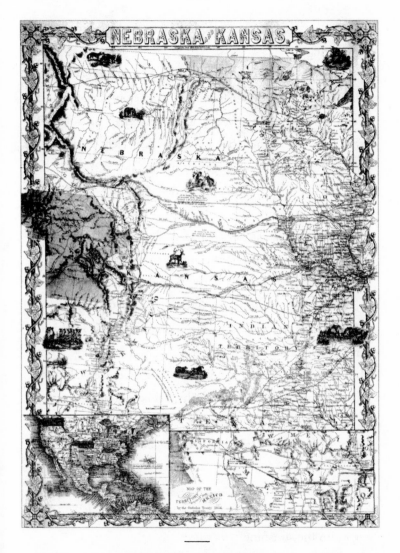

A map of the Kansas and Nebraska territories

Adam wouldn't even look. Said, "Just what are you suggesting?"

Jesse grinned. "What I'm saying, brother Daniel, is that we could sit on our stumps and lose our farm. Or—I could go out to this Cherry Creek and snap up some of that gold that's lying about. Pay the farm debt in double-quick time. Be free of Judge Fuslin fast."

"What do you know about digging gold?" demanded Adam.

"Go on, read it," cried Jesse. "They got gold with an ax, didn't they? A hatchet! Lord! A frying pan!"

"You'd have no idea where to look," Adam scoffed.

"Sure I do," said Jesse. "Says it's on this Cherry Creek, right off the South Platte River. Guess what else I learned in town? These Cherry Creek diggings are only seven hundred miles from here. *Seven hundred!* I bet we walk that far when we plow each day! Why, a fellow could travel out there on his hands—backward."

"Now, Jesse," said my ma, "for once you need to be serious."

"I am!" cried Jesse.

Pa shook his head. "Jesse," he said, "dreaming don't work in the sunshine."

Jesse offered him the paper. "Printed words don't lie."

"If a man set the type, they can!" growled Adam.

"Digging for gold," said my mother, "I remember people wanting to go to California years ago."

"And if we'd gone," I cried, unable to hold back my keenness, "we'd be rich now."

Adam snorted. "Or dead."

"I guess you'd prefer losing the farm," Jesse taunted.

Adam turned red.

"Would you just go way out there, *alone*?" Ma asked Jesse.

Jesse looked across the table and winked at me. "Little brother can come with me. That way, we'd get the gold twice as fast."

"I like that," I said, ready to gallop.

"Lot of good Early would do you," said Adam.

"He'd do just fine," said Jesse, making me feel good.

"It would cost plenty to get there," said Adam. "And we don't have anything to spare."

"I'll find it," said Jesse.

"How?" Adam challenged.

Jesse didn't answer that question.

Pa shook his head. "We're not going to lose the farm. No one is going anywhere."

End of discussion.

But over the next few days, Jesse and I shared other newspaper stories up in our room.

The Iowa *Democrat* wrote:

The excitement caused by the discovery of the Pike's Peak gold mines is still unabated. Every man has gold on his tongue. The first question one hears in the morning after coming downtown is, "What's the news from the gold diggings?"

There was one from the Kansas *Weekly Herald*:

Gold! Gold! Gold! Reliable reports concerning the recent gold discoveries in the vicinity of Pike's Peak still continue to arrive. Every trader or prospector coming from the region gives flattering accounts. The gold has been discovered in all the streams flowing from the mountains. Those who ought to know say that with the proper tools fifty dollars can be obtained per day.

Days did pass, but all Jesse would talk about was Pike's Peak. "Gold! Fifty dollars a day! Early," he kept saying, "it'd be so fine if I could save the farm. Not for Adam. For your ma and pa. For all they done for me."

"Adam gets the farm in the end," I reminded him.

"Sure," he said, "but he'd have to thank me for it, wouldn't he?"

And I said, "And we'd have enough left over to buy another farm just for us."

"We would, too!" he said, laughing. Then he got serious. "Early, I got to go!"

In fact, couple of nights later he got so restless he walked right out of the room we shared, and, so he told me later, sat on the porch all night staring at the moon.

Next morning all he said to me was, "Hey, Early. Ever notice how much the moon looks like gold?"

No doubt, Jesse had gold fever, and he had it bad. But what it would lead to, I had no idea.

CHAPTER FOUR

Hard Times, Strange Times

THE PEOPLE in our part of the country were getting desperate about money. All kinds of unusual things were being gossiped about. The Robinson family, having big debts, up and disappeared one night. No one knew where they went. The bank in Wiota, the one Judge Fuslin owned, was broken into and robbed. Three hundred dollars stolen! Then there was Tobias Elliot, from the other side of town, who got so hopeless he took his own life. And we kept hearing about people—people who had stayed in Cass County their whole lives—who just packed up and headed west to that Pike's Peak place, or to California or Oregon— places that promised ways to recover busted lives.

Then we had our own strange thing happen.

Judge Fuslin sent Pa a message telling him he must come see him at the bank, right away. Pa went. When he met with the judge, Fuslin announced that he was sure *Jesse* was the one had who had robbed his bank! Being county judge, he could have had Jesse arrested.

"Do you have some proof?" Pa asked.

"He was seen in town that night," said Fuslin. "Near the bank."

"Don't mean a thing," Pa said and got up to go.

"Hold on," said Fuslin. "I'll make a deal. You sell that farm to the railroad, and I'll make sure no charges are placed against Jesse."

"Why would you do that?"

"Look here, Daniel, I'll be honest. If you sell to the railroad, I'll get my share."

"More than three hundred, I'd guess," said Pa.

"Yes, sir. A lot more."

"In other words," said Pa, "sell the farm, or Jesse gets arrested."

"Just trying to be helpful."

"Judge Fuslin," said Pa, "that's what I'd call blackmail." He left, came home, and told us what was said.

I was shocked by the charge against Jesse. Outright horrified.

"He offer any proof that it was me?" asked Jesse.

Pa repeated what the judge had said.

That made Adam ask Jesse, "Were you there? *Did* you rob the bank?"

But then Ma cried, "Adam! Don't even say such a thing!"

"Have anything to say for yourself?" Pa said to Jesse.

Jesse shrugged, grinned, and said, "What am I supposed to do? Can't just sit around waiting for that judge to arrest me, can I?"

Ma said, "If you didn't do it, you're not going to be arrested. We're not going to lose the farm."

Pa added, "No one is going anywhere. And we're not going to talk about it anymore."

That was fine with me, especially since I noticed Jesse hadn't answered Adam's question.

A few days later, it being Saturday afternoon, Adam allowed Jesse and me to go off on our own. We went out into our woods, at the southern end of the farm, where we had a place on some rocks that was good for sitting and talking. We hunted there, too. In fact, Jesse had his rifle, and we were waiting for the pigeons to rise when he drew out a piece of paper.

"Hey, little brother, look here," he said. "Fella in town had a brand-new guidebook about that Pike's Peak gold. I copied a piece. Listen to this:

"Gold exists throughout all this region. It can be found anywhere—on the plains, in the

There were all kinds of guidebooks to the gold diggings. Just a few of them had really good information.

mountains, and by the streams. In fact, there is no end of the precious metal. Nature itself would seem to have turned into a most successful alchemist in converting the very sands of the streams to gold.

"Isn't that something grand?" said Jesse. When he looked at me with his bright eyes, I could have sworn I saw bits of gold swimming in them.

He stuffed the paper back in a pocket and picked up his rifle and aimed it. "I'm telling you, Early, I think I just might go see the elephant."

"Do *what?*"

"It's what folks say when they talk about going west: seeing the elephant."

"Are there *elephants* out there?"

"Doubt it. It's just what people say."

"Look here, Jesse," I said, "maybe you and me should go off and go see that elephant for ourselves. Get away from everyone."

"I just might," he said, lowering his gun. "I'm of age. But it wouldn't be fair to the folks to take you, little brother. Anyway, what'll Adam say?"

I said, "Don't care apple cores about Adam. Just don't

you go without me, Jesse Plockett. Anyway, didn't Adam say it cost money to go?"

Jesse thought for a moment. "About two hundred dollars."

"No way could we find that," I said.

"I might find a way."

I looked at him closely. "How?" I asked.

The only answer Jesse gave was to take aim, shoot, and drop a pigeon at forty yards. I always wanted to shoot like that.

"Wish that was old Fuslin," said Jesse. Then he added, "I saw him in town."

"He say anything?"

"Wanted to know if Daniel had thought about his offer. Said that time was running short."

"Before he places charges against you?"

"Sounded like."

"Jesse," I cried, "what you going to do?"

"Got some ideas," he said and shot another pigeon.

I will confess there were a whole lot of questions I wanted to ask him. First off: where was he that night he told me he was looking at the moon? Second: why did someone say he was seen in town that same night? I just couldn't get my words out. Kept putting them off for the morrow.

23

Then, a few days later when I woke and went down to the kitchen, Ma, Pa, and Adam were just there doing nothing. So right off I knew something had happened.

"What's the matter?" I asked.

"Jesse," said Adam.

"What about him?"

Pa handed me a piece of paper with Jesse's scrawl.

I'm going to the Kansas territory.
Just know I'll be bringing back some gold.
Jesse

"He gone?" I cried. "Really?"

Pa nodded. "Looking for gold."

"Fool's gold," added Adam.

Ma said, "He was fretting so about Judge Fuslin's charge that he thought he might as well go. Only took an extra shirt and his rifle."

"No money," said Pa, "and winter coming."

"Why didn't he tell me?" I said.

Ma shook her head and said, "I suspect he didn't want to disappoint you."

I was so upset, I ran off to our secret place in the

woods, hurt that Jesse would go without saying anything to me. But when I got there, I found another letter.

Little Brother:

I'm going to get some of that ~~that~~ Pike's Peak gold so as to pay off the mortgage and make everything right. Don't worry about me.
I'll be back soon rich as blazes. Don't let Adam bother you. We'll have our own farm soon!

Jesse

I spent a whole lot of time reading and rereading that letter, thinking about Jesse and what he'd done. He said I wasn't to worry about him, but I did. In fact, after I was finished brooding, I'd made up my mind: I had to go after him.

I just didn't know how.

CHAPTER FIVE

A Whole Lot of Time

October 1858

THREE WEEKS after Jesse left, we got a letter from him.

> *Dear Sister, Uncle, Early, and Adam:*
> *Got to Council Bluffs. People all excited.*
> *Say getting Pike's Peak gold is easy. Just*
> *there for picking up. Easy, Early, easy!*
> *   Jesse*

Meanwhile, Judge Fuslin sent word saying that Jesse's taking off proved he was guilty, so he was going to issue a warrant for his arrest. At the same time the judge again offered to drop charges if Pa sold him the farm.

Pa repeated his No.

Adam said, "Does Judge say he has any more proof that Jesse robbed the bank?"

"Just what he said before."

"Then there isn't any proof," said Ma, who like me, always did side with Jesse.

"I bet I know why Jesse went," said Adam. "An Iowa warrant isn't going to hold in the territories. Fuslin will have to send someone out there to drag him back."

I lost my temper. "You want him to be arrested, don't you!" I cried.

"You do something wrong, you pay for it," said Adam.

"He didn't do it!" I shouted.

"That's enough!" said Pa. "Things are difficult enough around here without you two snapping."

I went out and chopped some wood.

The next letter Jesse sent came two months later from a place called Fort Kearny. Somewhere out in the Nebraska Territory. This time all he wrote was:

I'm getting close!

Still, it proved he was on the move, still heading west.

Then for three *months* there was nothing but silence from Jesse. Not a single, solitary word.

"Might have died," said Adam.

I hated Adam for saying that. It made Ma cry, too. Pa told Adam to keep his thoughts to himself. All I could think about was how I was going to get out there and bring Jesse back.

Things went on, though it was dull without Jesse being about. Then, in March of 1859, another letter finally came from him.

> Dear Brother Daniel, Sister Penelope, Adam, + Early:
>   I got gold! Enough to pay our debt. But I am in danger from the blacklegs who would steal an honest man's hard diggings. My life is truly threatened!
>   Jesse
>   Cherry Creek Kansas Territory
>   January, 1859

I was real excited that Jesse got gold, but knowing he was in trouble made me wild. "Pa," I pleaded. "I have to go! Jesse needs me!"

"It's too dangerous," was all Pa said.

To which Adam added, "He should have listened to me."

Ma was upset, too, but she agreed. "Jesse will have to fend for himself. We need you on the farm, Early."

"If we don't help Jesse," I cried, "save his gold, clear his name, and pay our debts, this won't *be* our farm for long."

Adam said: "A king's ransom can't be paid by fool's gold."

"You just don't like him," I cried. "Always jealous of him. He was smart to leave!"

"Early," said Pa, "you are *not* going."

"Will too!" I cried, and skulked away, frustrated that I was the only one sticking up for Jesse.

But the truth was, even if I had had my parents' consent, I hardly knew how to get out to that Cherry Creek. There were those seven hundred miles to cross. Back then no trains were going west past the Missouri River. Far as I knew, a stagecoach had yet to commence running. To get there you had to walk, go by wagon, or ride an animal. I was stuck in Iowa.

But then, I got lucky.

CHAPTER SIX

I Find a Way

April 26, 1859

WHENEVER I could, I went to town with Pa, hoping to find another letter from Jesse. None came. Even so, I made certain to listen close because lots of people were talking about different ways of going west.

Mind, people talked a lot about going to Pike's Peak. Actually, it was Cherry Creek where the gold reports came from—a place some eighty miles *north* of Pike's Peak. I suppose there was something grand and powerful in a "peak," more than just a "creek."

What I learned was that Adam had one thing right: unless you had your own rig, or hired on, it took some two *hundred* dollars to pay your way to the diggings! Only one

I knew with that kind of money was Judge Fuslin.

So there I was, packed as tight with worry as a wadded-up musket ball. Just as ready to explode with frustration, too.

Then two things happened, one stupid, one lucky. The stupid one came first.

Pa asked me to go to town with a pig he'd fixed to sell to the butcher. I hitched our mule to our wagon, got Senator Clay (the pig) loaded, and clattered the six miles to town. Dealt with the pig, then walked toward the post office, hoping for a Jesse letter. But who should come along? Judge Fuslin.

Fuslin always dressed fine, with shiny black frock coat, vest, and neck cloth. His buffed top hat (black) made him seem tall. Liked his Cuban cigars, too. Mind, nothing wrong with any of it. But knowing the power he had over us, knowing the way he'd threatened Jesse, I held him low. He was my enemy.

There was a big man walking with him, someone I didn't know. So I didn't pay much mind to him—not then.

And when I spied Fuslin coming along, I admit, I walked right by him. Only, he hailed me.

"Early!" he called. "Early Wittcomb!"

Had to stop.

"Yes, sir?"

"I'm sure your parents would agree," he said, one hand gripping his jacket lapel like he was a politician giving a dull speech, "it's only polite to greet your elders."

He had me there. As my ma was forever saying, *Being rude means you're taking a rough road when you can just as well take a smooth one.* So I said, "Yes, sir. Sorry, sir. How do you do, sir?"

He considered me for a moment. "Any word about Jesse?"

Since he knew Jesse was gone, I took it he was really asking two things: where Jesse was, and whether Pa was talking about the deal he'd offered. I shouldn't have said anything, but I wanted to push back. So I said, "Yes, sir, we just got word from the Pike's Peak diggings. Guess what? Jesse's got gold. Buckets of it. Enough to pay our debts and then some." I suppose I grinned, too, as like to say, *We're going to keep the farm. And he's got away from you.*

Fuslin paled. "Has he?" the judge said. "I'd hate to haul him back to face those theft charges."

"Yes, sir," I said. "But I'm sure he'll be staying out there."

"He can be reached," Fuslin said.

The man by his side looked at me fierce, as if to back up anything the banker said.

"Yes, sir," I muttered and went off. I didn't think too much about it, because right after that meeting something lucky happened. I went on to the post office, where I didn't find a letter but something almost as good. Nailed to the wall was a notice:

PIKE'S PEAK!

Who wants to go to Pike's Peak without costing himself anything? As many as four young men, of good character, who can drive an ox team, will be accommodated by four gentlemen who will leave this vicinity on the 2nd of May. We can furnish you beds and board and have your washing and mending done: and you shall give us your help as we require to get our families and effects to Cherry Creek. We have four wagons.

Come on, boys!

Ebenezer T. Bunderly, esq.

I felt like giving a hoot, a holler, and three hurrahs.

There it was! A way to get to Pike's Peak and Jesse on my own without it costing a cent.

I skipped over to the postmaster and asked who this Mr. Bunderly fellow was and where I could find him.

"Bunderly? He's that new barber who just came to town. Set up behind Morton's Stables."

I'd heard about barbers, but since my ma cut our hair and trimmed my father's and Adam's beards, I had never actually met one. Always seemed odd to pay someone to do what you could do yourself—or have your ma do for you.

Anyway, I found the barber in a shack behind the stables off Main Street. The space, just a tiny room, poorly lit, contained a chair plus a small table on which lay scissors, shaving brush, mug, razors, a sharpening stone, and strop. There was also a washbasin and some hunks of gray soap.

Mr. Bunderly—I guessed it was him—was sitting in the chair, legs up, reading a slim pamphlet, blue covered. Its title: *The Emigrant's Guide to the South Platte and Pike's Peak Gold Mines.*

He was a tall weed of a man, all elbows and knees, with thin, reddish hair and beardless pink face. His hands, which held the pamphlet, were small, clean, and with no dirt under his nails, not looking as if they were used to

This picture reminds me of Mr. Bunderly's barbershop in Wiota.

much hard labor. You might say there was something pale and blurry about the man, almost watery.

"Yes, boy?" he inquired, peering at me with gray-blue eyes.

"Are you Mr. Bunderly?"

"At your service, sir. And I see you are in need of a haircut."

"No, sir, it's about your notice at the post office.

You're wanting some boys to go with you to Pike's Peak."

"I'm grateful for your inquiry, my boy, but the actual need is for young *men*."

"Yes, sir, only it did say, 'Come on, *boys*.'"

He put down his reading matter and considered me thoughtfully. "May I be so bold as to inquire as to your age?"

"Fourteen."

"An unfortunate orphan, perhaps?"

His saying that, and my knowing he'd just come to town so he most likely didn't know me, led me to do an awful and fateful thing: I lied shamefully. I said, "Yes, sir, I'm an orphan."

"How do you manage to survive?"

"Hire around."

"Do you have an abode to . . . sleep?"

"Nothing much. About five miles out of town."

His soft eyes gazed at me. "Not by any chance running away, are you?" he asked.

"Oh, no, sir!"

"Yet you desire to make the passage west?"

"Yes, sir, I do."

"Why is that?

"Get some of that Pike's Peak gold."

"I will allow"—he nodded—"it's what everyone says."

"Please, sir," I asked, "are you going to look for gold, too?"

"Like so many others, my boy, these days I am financially embarrassed. I had thought to put down roots here, but to remain is to insure absolute ruin. Accordingly, I have resolved to move on and try my fortune in the Pike's Peak region. Though I've little interest, or skill, in obtaining gold, it is my firm conviction that men of great wealth will desire their beards to be trimmed. Therefore, I shall put forward sufficient enterprise by which to mend my broken fortunes. I do believe, young man, that without endeavor there can be no progress—material or spiritual."

Mr. Bunderly really did talk like that—planting words all around his thoughts, rather than weeding them.

"Now, then," the barber said, "are you capable of hard labor? The rigors of a long and hazardous journey?"

"Yes, sir. I can drive an ox, gather eggs—and they don't break, neither—and muster a rifle. Danger don't dither me."

"Your name, young man?" he asked.

"Early, sir."

"Would that be surname or Christian name?"

"Works both ways," I replied.

He pursed his lips. "I fear I'm not entirely convinced as to your veracity."

I stood there, holding my eyes steady, hoping my silence could prop up the lie.

"Son," the barber finally said, "you create a quandary for me. In my wagon will be my ailing wife, and young daughter. On one hand, I suspect you are not being candid. On the other hand, having failed here, I am obligated to go, *now*, short-handed though I am. As I say, my wife does not enjoy robust health. Rock fever, I fear. As for my daughter, she is, shall we say, somewhat undisciplined. Lacking a mother's firm hand, I suspect. In conclusion, I am keenly in need of assistance. Shall I stand in judgment of you or take you at your word?"

"My word is pretty good, sir."

He sighed. "It hardly seems wise to commence a long-term arrangement when doubt is deep."

"I don't doubt you, sir," I put forward.

He grew thoughtful and gazed at me. "Mr. Early," he said at last, "what is your knowledge of women?"

"Women, sir?" I said, surprised by the question.

"My beloved wife can be . . . complex," he suggested. "And my daughter . . ." Words failed him. Then he said, "Miss Eliza is nobody's fool. She can skin a snake alive."

"I'm sure I'll treat them with respect, sir" was the best I could come up with.

He was silent for a while, then sighed and said, "Mr. Early, we intend to depart next week—Monday. In the morning."

"I can manage that, sir. I'm sure I can."

"You're absolutely positive you're free to go?" he asked.

"Yes, sir, I am."

He held up one of his fine hands as a caution. "Some conditions: We shall keep the Sunday Sabbath by not traveling. There will be no liquor, tobacco, or speaking with profanity. Can you abide by that?"

"Yes, sir."

"Today is Tuesday. I repeat: we leave Monday morning. And since no better prospects than you have come forward, I shall depend upon your being honorable."

"Oh, thank you, sir!" I cried. "You won't regret it, sir. You won't!"

I went outside and truly jumped into the air. "Goodbye, Judge Fuslin," I shouted. "Jesse! Here I come!"

CHAPTER SEVEN

I Leave Home

April 27–May 2

MY JOY did not last long. I was too weighed down by my sinful lies. Didn't matter that I told myself, *I'm doing it to help Jesse so he can save the farm.* I'd put forward an awful untruth, and I was about to run away from home and family. Hardly a wonder that as I made my way home, I was excited one moment, close to tears the next.

At the farm, everything looked strange to me, shaped and colored by my knowing I was about to depart. Though the farm was where I'd lived every day of my life, it was as if I were seeing it anew. If a boy can be homesick before leaving home, that was me.

It was unsettling, too, to be with Adam, Pa, and Ma

that night. My secret head kept thinking, *If only you knew what I was going to do.* The next moment, from some way they looked or said something to me, I'd think, *Jiminy! They've guessed my plan.*

Naturally, I wondered what they would think of my going. Naturally, I couldn't ask.

Over the next few days, I found myself wanting to throw my arms around Ma and say, *Forgive me for going. I have to help our Jesse. Give me your blessing before I go.*

Or I'd take note of Adam's scowl and think, *You're going to see what I can do when Jesse and I save the farm!*

When I looked at my pa, my thought was, *I'm doing this for the farm, Pa. Please understand.*

But not one word escaped my lips. I kept all within like a bunged-up barrel of rain in a long dry spell.

The night before I was to leave and we were all at the table, I was unable to contain myself. "I really think I should go help Jesse," I blurted out.

Adam frowned. "Early, how many times must we say it—you're needed here."

Pa added, "Costs money to go, Early. We've none to spare."

"With Fuslin after Jesse," said Ma, "maybe it's better he's gone."

"Do you think he robbed that bank?" I cried.

"We always think the best of Jesse," said Ma.

I gazed at them in wretched silence and thought, *What would you say if I told you I'd found a way to go for nothing and was leaving in the morning?* Oh, how much I wanted their consent that I might feel better about my leave-taking.

All I said, though, was "Jesse really needs me."

When no one replied, I cried, "He's in danger, isn't he? Don't that go for something?" My eyes welled with tears. "He says he got gold, didn't he? He only went to get it for us so we could pay our debts and save the farm. How's Adam going to inherit the farm 'less we can find a way to keep it? It's all for the family!"

"Early, no more!" snapped Adam. "You're too young to go! It's my job to find a way to save the farm."

His saying that righted things a bit. I yelled, "Jesse's done more than you!"

Ma reached out and put her rough hand on mine and said, "Early, Jesse will have to care for himself."

"Jesse's gone," agreed Pa. "No point talking about him."

So there was no more that night.

I got ready in secret. Wasn't no fuss to it. I'd wear leather boots, my baggy linen trousers, wool undershirt, and shirt. I stuffed an extra set of trousers and shirt in a flour sack. Winter being over, I wore no socks, but I did wear a vest, which had a fine pocket. I knew the clothing would hold up even for a rough journey since Ma had not only sewn them, she'd woven the cloth from which they'd been cut.

When I added my old broad-brimmed felt hat to keep sun and rain off my face, I was ready to go.

It was Monday, May 2, 1859, just before dawn when I got up. It had rained some the night before, so the air was sweet as gooseberry pie. But my heart was heavy, and I was sorely tempted to go where my parents lay abed and bid them a fair good-bye. Instead I left two notes. One, under my bed blanket, that read

WENT TO CHERRY CREEK TO RESCUE
JESSE AND BRING BACK THE GOLD.

EARLY

And another on the table.

GONE FISHING. EARLY

I hoped that that last one would keep them from

looking for me for a while—least till I was well gone.

With dawn just a pink promise in the eastern sky, I stepped from the house and began running down the road toward town. My heart was heavy, but my resolve high.

Would I have gone if I'd known what raw trials lay before me?

CHAPTER EIGHT

Lizzy

May 2, 1859

I GOT to Wiota as fast as I could, only to discover that many people had come out to watch the wagon-train leave-taking. Needing to make sure that the folks who knew me wouldn't guess what I was doing, I ambled about trying to look as if I was just curious. It was easy enough to find what I was seeking—four covered wagons lined up on the town's short main street. On one canvas wagon cover someone had boldly painted

PIKE'S PEAK OR BUST!

The wagons were about sixteen feet long, five feet

wide, built with white oak, and covered with rounded white canvas covers held up by hickory wood loops. Only one wagon looked new.

The canvas bonnet could be rolled up along the sides to let in air and had drawstrings front and back to keep out rain. Plus, the canvas was daubed with oil to make it waterproof. It was the whiteness of the sail-like covers and the slightly bowed bottoms of the wagons (to keep goods from rolling out) that made people call them "prairie schooners."

Each wagon had four large wooden wheels, which

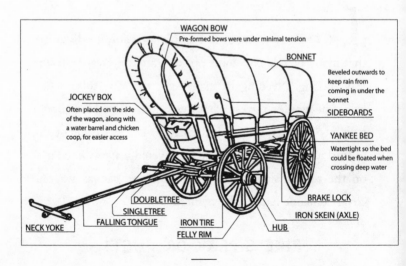

A good diagram of the kind of wagon the Bunderlys had.
They were strong, generally waterproof, and could float.

were rimmed with iron to make them last, with the front wheels smaller than the back ones and mounted on an axle that could be steered left and right. The brake lever was on the left side, reachable by the driver. The wheels turned on wooden axles, their hubs smeared with tar and fat to keep them moving cool and easy. If you didn't tar the hubs, the wheels screeched something awful. That's why a leather tar bucket was hung on the doubletree for easy access. In fact, some people called the wagons "tar grinders." Not nearly as pretty sounding as "prairie schooners," maybe, but I always thought that described them better.

Up front, harnessed to each wagon's tongue, were four yoked oxen. A pair of saddle horses was tethered to one wagon. Two milk cows were under the care of some young boys. A few chickens in cages were tied to another wagon. I even heard the squeal of a pig. The wagon train was a rolling barnyard.

I found Mr. Bunderly pouring drinking water into the barrel affixed to one side of his wagon.

"Ah, Mr. Early! How pleasant to know your name is equal to your promise," he said by way of greeting. "I bid you a most hearty welcome to our great adventure." He took my hand in his two and shook it as gravely as if I were joining a funeral procession.

Turning to the small woman seated on the front wagon seat, he said, "Dearest Mrs. Bunderly, this is the orphan boy—Early—I spoke to you about. He will accompany us and no doubt provide a great deal of useful assistance."

Mrs. Bunderly—dressed in formless, plain linen—peeked out from deep within her Shaker wire-framed bonnet. Her face, what I could see of it, was small and sallow, with large, anxious eyes. As it was, she barely looked at me, offering hardly more than a nod of acknowledgment, though she did extend a delicate hand that barely touched mine, only to withdraw as if fearful of contagion.

As Mr. Bunderly led me away, he whispered: "As I have already intimated, Mr. Early, my darling wife languishes in poor health. But I have heard reliable reports that the Cherry Creek air is sufficiently salubrious as to provide a potential remedy. We shall anticipate the best, shall we not? Enterprise feeds best on joy, not despair.

"Now, then, young man, you shall meet my daughter." We started off only to halt while he grasped my shoulder. "Do not," he whispered, "let her intimidate you."

Mr. Bunderly led me to a girl who was leaning against one of the large wagon wheels. She was gazing at me with much boldness.

"Mr. Early," said Bunderly, "this is my delightful daughter, Miss Eliza. Miss Eliza, this is the plucky orphan lad who will be offering us needful aid." That said, he walked away—in haste, I thought—leaving me alone with the girl.

She was a tall, skinny girl, dressed in a long, not-too-clean calico dress. No hoopskirt for her. Around her neck hung her bonnet in slovenly fashion. Her face had bold green eyes that were almost saucy and a smudged, pug nose. Her hair was long and as red as any I'd ever seen. Her boots, men's and neither left nor right, had wooden soles, and were surely too large, which made her taller than I was. Her hands were big, almost bony.

In short, she was no beauty. I guessed her to be about my age, though for all I knew she could have been much older.

"Pleased to meet you, Miss Eliza," I said, more to my toes than to her face.

"Mr. Early, I can't say I share that pleasure," she returned in a voice I thought excessively loud.

"Beg pardon?" I said, taken by surprise.

"My father has taken you on because he doesn't think I'm capable of anything. And my mother," she said, tossing her red hair back with a smart snap of her head—

a gesture I would come to see many times—"doesn't *want* me to be capable. She thinks capability is unladylike."

"I'm sure your father will know what to do," I murmured.

"Mr. Early," she said, "if there is bravery in ignorance, you may be sure I have the bravest family in the whole world. My father brings along a pepperbox pistol about which I'm sure he knows not where the six bullets fit."

I stood there like a lump of mud.

"Do you know about guns?"

I shrugged. "My uncle taught me to use a rifle."

"Mr. Early," she said, giving me a rude poke in the ribs, "my pa said you're an orphan."

"Yes, ma'am, I told him that," was my careful reply.

She studied me, then said, "Mr. Early, I'm inclined to be interested in you."

"Why's that?" I asked.

She reached forward, took firm hold of my arm, drew me close, leaned down, and whispered into my ear, "Mr. Early, I've seen you about town with a man who bore a remarkable resemblance to being your father. I suspect you are no more an orphan than I. Indeed, I believe you *are* running away and therefore a brazen liar."

I pulled back, shocked.

Miss Eliza giggled at my reaction and added, "But, Mr. Early, you should know I find liars most entertaining, for they have deep secrets. I shall keep yours to myself."

"Th-thank you . . . Miss Eliza," I stammered.

"We'll talk again, Mr. Early, I'm sure," she said. "And if you desire my friendship, you shall never, *ever* call me Miss Eliza—I answer to Lizzy and nothing else." With a toss of her hair and a smirk, she walked away.

All I could do was look after her, aware that my face had grown hot, red, and stupid. Worse, if she knew about me, perhaps others would.

CHAPTER NINE

Westward, Ho!

BEFORE I could collect my wits, Mr. Bunderly reappeared. "And what do you think of my daughter, Mr. Early?" he asked.

"Most agreeable," I mumbled, hardly knowing what else to say.

"Indeed!" he returned. "I can think of many words to describe Miss Eliza, but I doubt *agreeable* is to be found in her dictionary."

He went on to inform me that his plan was to go directly from our town to Council Bluffs. Once there, we would join with a bigger wagon train, then leave immediately for the diggings.

All I knew about Council Bluffs was that it was over in Pottawattamie County, maybe forty miles from Cass County, sitting on the eastern shore of the Missouri River. It's where Jesse's first letter had come from. Getting there would put me farther from home than I'd ever dreamed.

Next Mr. Bunderly led me to meet the three other families who would be in the train. They all had young

When people back East thought of the wagons going west, they concocted really pretty pictures.

children, which explained their need for extra, older hands. There was a Mr. Griffin, his wife, and son; Mr. Wynkoop, his wife, and three daughters; and a Mr. Hicksby, his wife, and two young sons, twins.

Then there were those who were being taken along like me—to work the train. They were a Mr. Tecknor, a Mr. Armon, and a Mr. Mawr. These men looked to be in their twenties, so among the extra hands, I was by far the youngest.

As I was to learn, all of these folks came from out of town but about Cass County, coming together for convenience. It meant my fear that I would be known was much reduced.

There was one exception. When Mr. Bunderly introduced me, Mr. Mawr looked somewhat familiar, but I didn't think it out, not then. I was too anxious and excited, wishing we would leave. Though I was as yet unrecognized, every slow-passing minute had me half expecting Adam or Pa might appear and haul me home.

So, midst the fussing with this and that on the wagons, getting them ready, adjusting the yoked oxen, loading children and chickens, I was doing two things: trying to keep out of sight, while wanting to act as grown up as I could, particularly in case Miss Lizzy might be observing me.

I stayed therefore as close to the Bunderly wagon as possible, keeping my hat brim low. I even thought of getting into the wagon to hide. But when I stole a look, I found it was stuffed helter-skelter with boxes, barrels, blankets, a feather bed, and tools—even a pig—so many things I could hardly tell what was in there, much less find a place to hide.

As I would learn, Mr. Bunderly had brought along some four hundred pounds of corn flour, one hundred of sugar, seventy of rice, and two hundred and fifty pounds of bacon, plus beans, coffee, molasses, and some dried fruit. I saw a Dutch oven—in which sat a six-barrel pepperbox pistol—and a tin coffeepot. An old Bible, blankets, and some medical ointments were there, plus more, too much and varied to enumerate. All had been set about in no particular design or order.

But as I turned from the wagon, I saw something disturbing: among the people who had come to see us off was Judge Fuslin. And he was staring at me.

I turned away in haste and dove behind the wagon. Then I peeped around to observe the judge speaking to one of the men who was coming with us, Mr. Mawr. Only then did I recollect where I'd seen him before: he'd been with the judge when I had told him about Jesse. I had little doubt Fuslin understood my intentions: I was going west with the train to be with Jesse. My stomach must have turned six times. Being in the train meant I'd be leading his friend, this Mr. Mawr, right to Jesse. Oh, how I regretted bragging to the judge!

I was still wondering what to do when one of the wagon drivers—Mr. Wynkoop—yelled, "Let's get a-going!"

That was when old Reverend Gideon Fobbscott from our Episcopal Methodist Church, a white-bearded fellow in black frock coat, stepped forward. "Neighbors!" he cried in his rough, booming voice. "I should like to bestow a final blessing upon our emigrant friends!"

People quieted down as the minister stepped up on a porch that overlooked the wagon train. He then commenced his preaching. He went on for a time, and I'll confess, wanting to leave as quickly as possible, I paid but scant attention. Still, in the middle of his sermon he said something that I would never forget.

He said: "Gold looks like a god's eye, bright, bold, and beautiful. It's smooth and soft, the way a god's touch should feel. You can bend it, shape it, and darn near chew it. It won't change on you. It won't rust. Get enough gold in your hands, and you can buy yourself a palace.

"But," cried the minister, and it seemed as if he was

pointing his stubby finger right at me, "gold can make a person crazy. Because if you get gold seeping into your heart and mind, if you let it take over your soul, it will turn you into a hard devil. The only thing your gold can buy you then is a cold coffin in a colder grave."

His words chilled my heart.

Next moment Mr. Wynkoop called, "Westward ho! Gee!" and cracked a long bullwhip over his oxen team. The great beasts leaned into their yokes. One bellowed. Wheels groaned but turned. Wagons lurched. Wood and leather creaked. As we began to roll forward, the crowd shouted, "Godspeed!" "Farewell!"

I felt true distress at leaving my parents behind in such a fashion. And what was I to do about Mr. Mawr? Was I to be a stalking horse, leading him straight to Jesse? I didn't think he had ever seen Jesse, but no doubt Judge Fuslin provided a description.

Not sure whether to stay or go, I stood in the middle of the road, only to feel a pluck upon my sleeve. I turned, and there was Lizzy.

"Orphan boy," she taunted. "Ain't you coming, after all? Did I scare you off?"

"I'm coming," I murmured and hastened to catch up with the wagons.

Laughing, the red-haired girl ran ahead of me, scrambled onto the tailgate of her wagon, and watched me run. She even stuck out her tongue at me.

One of our wagon owners, Mr. Griffin, and his son, Peter, had fife and drum, and led the way out of town playing a stirring "Yankee Doodle." The crowd cheered. It was like the glorious Fourth of July!

The music quickened my steps and allowed me to show some spirit, though I will, in the name of honesty, admit to feeling a mix of joy and sickness all at once.

"Jesse," I whispered to myself by way of encouragement, "hang on! I'm a-coming to see the elephant!"

CHAPTER TEN

We Head West

I

T WAS almost noon when we got going, taking the road that led west from Wiota. Mr. Bunderly asked me to walk beside his oxen team (with a prod stick). He sat in the driver's seat, reins in hands, his sad-eyed wife by his side. Miss Eliza began in the wagon, but she soon got out and started walking by my side, talking nonstop about her pet pig, Apollo, who trotted at our heels. She told me all about what she hoped to do out in the Cherry Creek diggings.

When I gave but scant reply, she fell into silence.

"Mr. Early?" she suddenly asked. "Do you not care for young ladies?"

I felt my face grow hot. "Don't know anything about them."

She made a quick glance back at her parents, and then she whispered, "Mr. Early, my mother keeps telling me to be ladylike, but I say it will only prove to be a hindrance in the uncivilized lands to which we go. Have you any opinion on that subject?"

Hardly knowing what to say, I fetched up with, "I suppose you're fine the way you are."

She laughed, tossed her red hair back, scooped up the squealing pig, and left me.

No, sir, I hardly knew what to think of such a creature.

The weather proved decent when we began, but in late afternoon a violent rainstorm came down. My first thought was that was good for our farm. In haste, I helped us camp near a village whose name I didn't know. I don't think we had gone but five miles.

When the storm passed over, lightning cracked close enough to send the milk cows scattering. I was told to go after them, which I did. When I had led them back, I was asked to light a fire in the rain so a meal could be cooked. It took a while, but I did that, too. That's when I began to grasp how little Mrs. Bunderly, with her poor health, would do. But since it was considered women's work to do the cooking, Lizzy—without complaints—was the one who dodged the smoke and set forth the bacon, corn cake, beans, and coffee, which were good enough. She took pains to feed her mother first.

Chores done, I crawled beneath the wagon on the wet ground and wrapped myself in a blanket provided by Mr. Bunderly, for such was the bed he had promised in his notice.

Lizzy, who had brought the blanket to me, squatted down and peered in. "Wish they'd let me sleep under here," she announced, before retiring to the comfort of the wagon.

I began to consider that she might be daft.

May 3

The day dawned agreeably and so we started early. Then one of the wagons (Mr. Hicksby's) had to stay back so his brake lever could be adjusted. Mr. Mawr showed himself to be a forceful man. Though he was a hired hand, he debated with Mr. Wynkoop, insisting we move forward. Mr. Bunderly took no part in the debate. Whether Mr. Mawr was right or wrong, I don't know; but his will prevailed, and we went on.

I kept alert regarding this Mr. Mawr. He was a large, imposing man with broad shoulders, clean shaven enough to show a constant scowl. Dressed himself in buckskin. Now and again he took note of me, a nod here and there, but we exchanged no words. That was fine with me. I tried to convince myself that perhaps I was wrong: that he had no particular interest in me or Jesse.

All told, that second day we went about seven miles and camped near a slow creek.

May 4

Shortly after we started, we came upon a half-mile of marsh. Though we tried to go forward, our wagons sunk up to their axles. We had to wait till Mr. Hicksby's wagon joined us. He grumbled and said we should have waited before starting across the marsh. In the end we had to empty the wagons, then haul long and hard to pull the wagons forward one at a time. Then reload them. Miss Eliza helped.

That day I believe we did not go a mile.

It was odd to be with strangers all the time. I'd forget their names, or they mine. Different ways of talking, too. I said "bucket." Mr. Griffin said "pail." Mrs. Wynkoop was wont to complain about hardship. You had to stand close to Mr. Hicksby to hear his soft talking. In the miles we had gone, it felt as if I had gone to a different world.

May 5

Got moving, only to strike another low marsh, in which the teams were stuck fast yet again. It was powerful work to get them out—eight oxen to pull each wagon through. Then the road that followed was poor. Happily, the next creek we came to had a bridge. That was progress. Still, here it was just a few days from starting, and already I began to wonder how long our journey to Cherry Creek would take. A long while, I reckoned. I hoped that Jesse could wait for me.

As we wore on, I chanced to note that Mr. Mawr carried a Colt pistol on his belt. What need, I wondered, required him to have a fancy weapon like that?

May 6

The weather proved fine, but we soon reached a big creek that was flooded some fifty yards wide, so we couldn't cross. Mr. Armon (a pleasant man) and I waded waist deep until we found a shallow spot. Then we drove the wagons across. At one point our wagon was afloat, the oxen swimming. All proved secure.

Such was our relief that when we got to the town of Marengo, Mr. Griffin and his son, Peter, led the way, playing "Oh! Susanna" in lively fashion. My heart was lightened.

That night when I crawled under the wagon to sleep,

Crossing streams and creeks was always a tricky business.

Lizzy appeared again and peeked in at me.

"Mr. Early?"

"Look here," I said, propping myself up on one elbow, "you don't want that name 'Miss Eliza.' Well, I don't want you calling me 'Mister.'"

She laughed. "I thought I was being respectful."

"Sounds otherwise," I said.

"But, Mr. Early—"

"I'm not talking to you if you call me that."

She stared at me for a moment and seemed to make a decision. "Early," she said, "can I tell you something?"

"You can say what you want."

"Then I so want to know why you are running away from your family."

I hardly knew what to say. "Why do you need to know?"

"I *hate* not knowing things," she said.

Though much annoyed, I grumbled, "I'm not running away."

"You are doing *something* devious."

"I'm going to Cherry Creek."

"You grow up in that town, Wiota?"

I nodded. "Nearby."

She was quiet for a moment, sat down on the ground,

and then drew up her knees and hugged them. "We were there only a month. You won't believe how often we've moved. My mother didn't want to go. Says she's too ill with her fevers."

"Is she?"

Lizzy nodded. "Rock fever. Brings waves of heat and unhappiness. Hurts right into her bones something awful. But my father said we had to go, as it is our last chance."

"Chance for what?"

"To restore health to his business and to my ma. She insists she'll not live to get there." Lizzy paused again before saying, "Mr. Early, I envy you."

I sighed. "Why?"

"I'd like to run away from my family."

"Why would you want that?"

"Then I could do all kinds of things."

"What kinds of things?"

"Get gold for myself," she said. "Be the richest lady on the whole earth."

"If you went to sleep," I suggested, "you could dream about it."

She considered my remark and then said, "Early, I don't usually care for boys, but you're a mite sharper than most."

Next moment we heard her mother calling, "Miss Eliza! Where are you? I need you!"

She sighed. "Being an orphan seems fine to me."

She hastened away.

May 7

Crossed a river (I never learned its name) by pole ferry, the owner of which charged us one dollar each team. No less than robbery!

Made good miles, but then the men got into a dispute about when to stop. No one asked my opinion. In the end, we pushed on.

That same evening, Mr. Mawr finally spoke to me. I was tying down our ox team. When I looked up, there he was, staring down at me, full of scorn.

"Boy, what's your name?" he asked, as if he didn't know.

"Early."

He said, "Early, I have heard your uncle has already gone to the diggings."

Of course he'd heard. He was with the judge when I told him. He must have thought I hadn't recognized him.

"Maybe," I said.

"Going to meet him?"

"Could be."

"And he's done well, I suppose."

"I don't know that for certain," I replied, not pleased with the drift of his questions.

"Mr. Early," he said, "there is much that is uncertain in this world."

Any hopes I had that he was not interested in Jesse vanished: his words were a warning.

CHAPTER ELEVEN

Mr. Mawr

May 8, 1859

IT BEING Sunday, we rested—though we really had not gone very far. But the Lord will be served, even going west.

Mr. Griffin and his son, Peter, played fife and drum, and so we sang some old hymns. Lizzy, for such a tomboyish creature, surprised me with a fine voice. The songs she sang, one of which was "Home Sweet Home," filled me with affecting thoughts of our farm.

Had some dried fruit soaked in water as a Sunday treat.

May 9

In the morning, we were held up by a strong rain. Mr. Bunderly urged me to join his family as they huddled in the wagon. The rain beat on the canvas as if it were a drum, and there was some leaking. Thunder rumbled near. When lightning came the canvas lit up like a magic lantern. Apollo, Lizzy's pig, rested his head in her lap and now and again grunted. When he did, Lizzy looked at me, and we struggled to keep from laughing.

Mr. Bunderly sighed and said, "Laughter, as the poet said, is the soul of youth turned to sound."

"Don't you ever laugh, Mr. Bunderly?" I asked.

"Mr. Early, consider: I now reside in a wagon with all my earthly possessions, my beloved wife and daughter, and you, Mr. Early—plus a pig. Outside, a deluge. A genuine summation of what my existence—so far—has achieved." He spoke with such solemnity that Lizzy and I could not hold back our laughter.

"Miss Eliza!" cried Mrs. Bunderly. "Be a lady!"

The poor woman spread her misery.

When the rain cleared, we discovered one team of oxen had strayed, so our start was late. That said, we went six miles, but stopped when we found some old fence posts. I set them to fire while, as usual, Lizzy cooked our dinner: bacon, rice, corn cake, and coffee.

Eating with the Bunderlys was not like eating with my family. My family talked and argued—at least Jesse and Adam did. And there was no better bread than my mother's. But at camp, Mrs. Bunderly rarely spoke, save to criticize Lizzy. Their corn cake was heavy. Mr. Bunderly gave long speeches, which made Lizzy roll her eyes or appeal to me with impish looks.

I missed my family.

May 10

We continued on. The slowness of our progress weighed on me. I worried much about Jesse and his predicament. Then I reminded myself that worry would not move me faster. All I could do was keep going. But I could not keep from fretting about Mr. Mawr.

At one point Lizzy walked by my side, her long skirt dragging in the muddy road, her bonnet, as usual, dangling down her back.

"Early, you mustn't be bothered by my mother. She can't scold her illness, so she scolds me. I try not to mind."

"It's all right," I said.

We went on in silence for a bit and then she said, "Early, I so do wish to know why you are going to the diggings."

I considered her question, shrugged, and said, "Same as everyone else. To get the gold."

"Early," she said, "by now you should know that I will take pride in keeping your secrets." She put a hand to her heart as proof.

I glanced at her sideways. She was looking at me, too. "A shared secret is an honor shared," she said, trying to make her words solemn. Next moment she sputtered and laughed. "When I talk like Father, I sound thick."

I returned her honesty by blurting out, "I've an uncle at Cherry Creek."

"Does he know you're coming to him?"

I shook my head.

"He get any gold?"

"Think so."

"He going to give you some?"

"Don't know."

She considered my reply and then said, "I should like you to know, I shan't marry unless the man is rich."

"Why is that?"

"Rich people do as they choose."

"Can rich wives?" I asked.

She glared at me and tossed her hair. "I will."

"Fine, then. And what would you do?"

She thought a bit and finally said, "Not sure." Then, as if correcting herself, she added, "But I'd do it."

For some reason or other, we both laughed. It felt good to do so.

We went on for a while, and then she said, "I hate this stupid bonnet."

"Why wear it, then?"

"Ma doesn't want me looking dark."

"Dark is better than washed-out and peaked."

For once it seemed as if I had surprised her. "Do you truly think so?"

"Just said, didn't I?"

After a moment she whipped her bonnet off, looked round at me, and grinned.

I was pleased we were becoming easy.

May 11

Went twenty miles, which was the most we had gone in one day. Toward sunset, we found a sinkhole with good water.

If you look at this picture, you can see some wagons were pulled by oxen, others by mules. Sometimes, even by horses. Oxen were considered best, being strongest, and because they really liked to eat the prairie grass.

Lizzy served up bacon, beans, corn cake with molasses, and coffee. I was tempted to ask if she could cook anything else. Didn't.

In the evening, when I crawled under our wagon as I usually did to sleep, I found myself restless. As I lay there, I heard footsteps approach our wagon.

"Mr. Bunderly?" a voice called.

"Is that you, Mr. Mawr? Good evening." It was Mrs. Bunderly who had replied.

"Evening, ma'am. I hope you're feeling better."

"I do the best I can."

"Mrs. Bunderly, I was wanting to speak to your husband about that boy of yours, Early."

"My husband is asleep. Is there something I can answer for you?"

"I heard say the boy is traveling to meet his uncle in the diggings. Has he spoken of that to you?"

"He told my husband he's an orphan, that's all."

"Did he? Has he said why he's going out to this uncle?"

"Not to me," said Mrs. Bunderly.

"I wonder if he can be trusted," said Mr. Mawr. "You might be better without him. You can find another in Council Bluffs."

"You can speak to my husband in the morning or even with my daughter. She's on good terms with the boy."

"With your permission, I shall. Good night."

"Good night, Mr. Mawr."

I hated that man.

CHAPTER TWELVE

News About Jesse

May 12

I WOKE TO discover our oxen had broken loose again. Mr. Bunderly had not tied them properly. Since we could not move without, I had to find them. When I did and yoked them up, I offered to tie up the oxen from then on. Afterward we went along a road of black mud.

As we went, I kept wondering if Mr. Mawr had spoken to Mr. Bunderly and what he might have told him. If he had, the barber said nothing to me about it. That eased me somewhat. But since Mawr might speak to Lizzy, too, and she being so unpredictable, I still worried.

May 13

That day we went only three miles but reached the Nishnabotna River, where we camped. I took Lizzy fishing and got ourselves a catfish. I even cooked it for her.

She watched intently. "I never saw a man cook before," she said.

"I'm a boy."

"Does that mean, Mr. Early, you're going to stop when you get older?"

"Why must you always ask outlandish questions?" I said.

She tossed her hair. "I only ask what I wish to know." Her green eyes seemed fierce.

"Need you know so much?"

"Are you comfortable with ignorance?"

"A body can't know everything."

"Mr. Early, I believe it's time you started thinking."

"Why's that?"

"Knowing everything is impossible. But knowing nothing is despicable."

Unable to argue, I made no reply.

As the fish was cooking, she said, "Early, why doesn't Mr. Mawr like you?"

"Don't he?"

"He was asking questions about you."

"Like what?"

"He suggests there are doubtful aspects to your life."

"Does he?"

"So when he asked me about you, I told him I knew your great secret."

"You did?" I cried.

"I confided to him that you were the concealed, if unnatural, son of the Emperor Bonaparte."

"You didn't!"

"Did," said a grinning Lizzy. "I will say I don't care for Mr. Mawr."

"Me neither."

Then she said, "You haven't noticed."

"What?"

"Since I threw away my bonnet—the result."

"What?"

"Freckles."

I looked over and said, "I think you look pretty fine."

For once, I detected something like a blush.

May 14

We forded Silver Creek near the town of Latimer's Grove.
When we got to the other side, we came upon a camp of
some fifteen wagons, all going to the Cherry Creek mines.

That evening, when the men sat around the fire as they
did most nights, there was much talk about Pike's Peak.

Lizzy and I sat out on the edge and listened.

All the men agreed that the gold in Cherry Creek

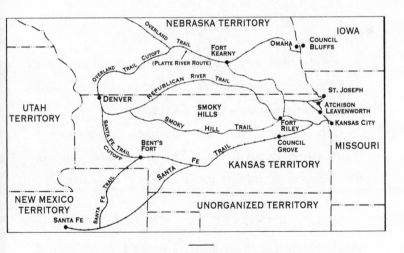

A really clear map showing the various trails out to the Pike's Peak
diggings. When the state of Colorado was organized, it was made from
parts of the Kansas, Nebraska, Utah, and New Mexico territories.

was plentiful. Much talk, too, about the best route to get to the place. Some championed the Platte River route. Mr. Wynkoop insisted that the Republican River trail was most favorable. Mr. Griffin mentioned something called the Smoky Hill route as the shortest.

There seemed as many points of view as sparks flying from the fire. But in all the arguments it occurred to me that no one really knew. That part was like the fire's smoke.

That so many grown men could go so far for so long without knowing the best way startled me.

May 15

It being Sunday, we rested. The weather was fine. Some took the time to cast some shot for their guns. Some baked bread. I wished Lizzy would do the same.

I heard Mrs. Bunderly complain loudly about her health. Mr. Bunderly tried to soothe her. She scolded him for being a fool, and then told Lizzy she was slatternly.

The girl stomped off.

Shortly after, Mr. Mawr came along and ordered me to watch the cattle. Sunday or not, I suppose somebody had to do it, and I was the youngest of the hired hands. So although Mr. Mawr was surly with me, I went all the same.

Apollo trotting by her side, Lizzy found me. The girl said nothing but sat on the ground and watched over the cows with me. "It being Sunday," she suddenly announced, "I'll sing you hymns."

She did, too: the old Methodist song "How Can We Sinners Know," and then "Our Ancient Fathers."

When she was done, I said, "You've got a real fine voice."

She said nothing to my compliment but then said, "Early, what do you think of bloomer suits?"

"Can't say I know what they are."

"Some lady by the name of Miss Bloomer invented them for ladies to wear beneath their skirts. So they might walk and run."

"Ladies aren't supposed to run."

"I like to."

I looked at her and grinned. "Then you'd best wear bloomers."

She giggled and said, "I think I just may."

Next moment she

A Bloomer girl! I'm not sure how Lizzy would have looked.

sang "Hark, the Herald Angels Sing," while hugging her pig, who grunted. I suspected she taught the pig to do so.

I never knew what Lizzy would do next.

May 16

We crossed another creek.

Having yet to ride in the wagon, I began to wonder if I would walk the whole way.

By the road we came upon a crude gravestone. It read:

GEORGE W. RIPLEY
HARTFORD, CONNECTICUT
DIED OF A FEVER, 1859
AGE 6
RIP

Lizzy said, "Early, I will pray that his journey to paradise is nearer than Connecticut."

The grave put us in a somber mood.

May 17

We went eight miles, and by crossing Keg Creek came within ten miles of Council Bluffs—or so I was told. That evening we found a camp of some eight wagons. One wagon had these familiar words on its canvas:

PIKE'S PEAK OR BUST!

But someone had crossed off the first three words, then added some letters so that it read

BUSTED BY THUNDER

We discovered that these people, all men, looking

A "go-backer" or "stampeder," heading back East—if he can make it.

weary and sadly worn, were coming *back* from the Pike's Peak diggings, going home to Ohio state. I was shocked.

We made camp nearby, for naturally we wanted to learn their story.

The men of our train—with Lizzy and me—approached their camp and introduced themselves.

It was Mr. Bunderly who said, "Gentlemen, we've only just begun heading toward the Kansas mining territory and would be pleased to gain from your experiences."

These Ohio men, twenty-four in all, were sullen and seemed reluctant to speak. But then one of them said, "Mister, if you want the truth, it's this: you are fools to go there."

"There's no gold to be had in Cherry Creek," said another.

"Nothing?" said Mr. Mawr.

"Nothing."

"But—"

"We've been there," said another. "It's all a humbug. A pack of lies."

We pressed them for particulars, but the Ohioans would say little, other than to repeat what they had already said.

Our group retreated, but I stayed behind. There was

one old grizzled man in the returning train who kept himself somewhat apart. I went up to him.

"Sir," I ventured, "when you were out at the Cherry Creek mines did you ever meet a man by the name of Jesse Plockett?"

"Jesse Plockett?" he returned, his bleary eyes much more alert than before.

"Yes, sir."

"What makes you ask about him?"

"He's my near relation."

"Is he now?" He studied me for a while. "Fancy that. You going out to him?"

"Yes, sir. Is he alive and well?" I asked.

"Alive? Last I heard, he was. As for being well . . . I couldn't rightly say."

"Why?" I asked, alarmed.

The man seemed to consider his words. Then he said, "They say he killed a man."

"*Killed a man*! What happened?"

"Can't say I know for sure."

No matter how I pressed him he would add nothing. I went back to our camp greatly agitated. The things people were saying about Jesse! That he was a robber. A murderer. All I had to do was close my eyes and I'd see his wild golden hair, his walk, and that smile which always made me glad. I could hear his easy, laughing talk, too. No, what people said was not the Jesse I knew. And since I had no doubt that Jesse had gotten gold, I decided these men were wrongheaded about all the rest they said, too.

When I got back to our camp I was relieved to see that the men did not believe the go-backers either. We would press on.

When I returned to our wagon, Lizzy came up to me. "What were you asking that man back there?"

"Nothing much."

"Mr. Early," she shouted after me, "there are times Apollo says more than you!"

May 18

Started at dawn and worked our way up and down through a valley, then up some hills, from which we saw Council Bluffs city. Beyond was the great Missouri River. Knowing that when we crossed the river we would be in the Kansas Territory, I became greatly excited!

We had made progress, after all.

CHAPTER THIRTEEN

Farewell to Iowa

COUNCIL BLUFFS was the biggest town I'd ever seen. A fellow told me that some two *thousand* people lived there. Plus, the city was stuffed with emigrants (mostly young men, but some women, too), in hundreds of wagons and tents, along with oxen, mules, and horses. I'd never believed you could fit so many people and beasts in one place, a small valley between sandy bluffs that overlooked the Missouri River.

Seemed most everybody was going to Pike's Peak. But to get any farther west you had to cross the river. That meant, as some folks said, "leaving civilization."

There were three ferries, which went back and forth

Try counting the wagons here, and you'll sense just how many
there were waiting to cross the river.

all day. Even so, they weren't enough to carry all the
people and wagons wanting to cross. It was like water
backing up behind a beaver dam. All we could do was get
in line and wait to take our turn.

Our team chose the middle ferry (because that's where
we hauled up), a steam side-paddle boat called *The Nebraska
Number One*. It could (and did!) carry twelve wagons with
their teams, making thirty to forty crossings each day!

May 19

Waiting for our turn left plenty of time to do nothing. I
decided to look about Council Bluffs, so I asked Mrs.

Bunderly for permission to take Lizzy with me.

"Mr. Early," she returned, "I'm not sure it will be safe. Speak to Mr. Bunderly."

When I repeated her words to him, Mr. Bunderly said, "Alas, Mr. Early, my good wife does poorly today. When pain obscures her world, melancholy holds her heart. I worry about her much. But," he added, forcing a smile, "better grin than grimace.

"As for Miss Eliza, by all means, let her accompany you. But be prudent, Mr. Early, prudent! Do not fail me or her unfortunate mother in protecting the girl. She is the jewel in our otherwise lusterless crown."

Having received permission, I asked Lizzy to come with me, for which I was given a fine look which gratified me. So we set forth, me being mostly quiet, she chattering and commenting on all we saw. I never knew one to so love *seeing*.

But then, Council Bluffs was a whirligig of gold fever. Crowds of people tramping about on the dusty, deep-rutted main street, a never-ending market of men selling, buying or trading the most amazing things. Lizzy pointed out a man offering a barrowload of ladies' silk shoes in exchange for shovels. Beaver pelts swapped for axes. Five dollars for a wheelbarrow. Four for a hatchet!

It seemed like every commercial establishment we saw bore a name like "Pike's Peak Hotel," or "Pike's Peak Outfits," or "Pike's Peak Lunch." I imagined that if they could have branded water, there would have been "Pike's Peak Water." Lizzy even bought some "Pike's Peak Candy Nuggets" with a three-penny coin she had. They proved sweetly sour.

Voices filled the air, all of them, it seemed, speaking about Pike's Peak. Pike's Peak this, Pike's Peak that. Much of the talk was furious argument about which way to go. *How* to go—by wagon, handcarts, or just plain walking. There were arguments about *if* to go, as well. Though most wanted to get to Pike's Peak, some were going to the California diggings. Or to Oregon, which had just become a state. There was even a group of Mormons going to Salt Lake. Someone told us they had come from a country called Denmark. They surely spoke no language I knew.

We paused to observe a man standing on a soapbox, barking at a jeering crowd.

"Friends!" he cried. "There's no gold to be found at Pike's Peak!" He kept shouting. "It's all a fraud! A lie! A humbug! All made up by these river towns, who want to take our money and leave us to rot in the desert! I've been there. There is nothing!"

Prospectors often kept their gold dust in hollow feather quills.

A man held up a small cloth bag. "I found some!"

The crowd cheered. Whether the man actually did or did not have gold, we never knew for sure. But how I wished it had been Jesse!

There was a terrible amount of drinking (I had never seen so many saloons), gambling, and profanity right on the streets. Enough to make the devil blush. I was nervous about Lizzy, but she remained calm until she cried, "Look!"

I turned toward where she pointed, and saw two

women pass by dressed in rough jackets and what looked to be oversize, almost billowy trousers beneath their skirts.

"Bloomers!" said Lizzy with great admiration.

It was a world such as I had never seen before.

As we continued to wander through the crowds, I chanced to observe Mr. Mawr. Being so big, he was hard to miss, but I was sure he had not seen us. There being something purposeful in his walk, I wanted to follow him.

"Lizzy," I whispered. "It's Mr. Mawr. I need to see where he's going."

"Why?"

"Just follow!"

Though the crowds were thick, he wasn't difficult to follow. We watched when he went into a small building that bore the sign:

CHICAGO AND NORTH
WESTERN RAILWAY

Seeing it, I gasped.

"What's wrong?" Lizzy asked.

"Come with me," I said, grabbing her hand and leading the way out of town until we sat on one of the bluffs overlooking the river. I was so upset, I put all my caution aside and told Lizzy my story from the beginning: the rail-road wanting to buy our farm; our fear of losing the farm to foreclosure; Judge Fuslin accusing Jesse of robbing the bank; Jesse going off to the diggings in search of gold to pay that debt; his message; the judge's connection to Mr. Mawr; even what the go-backer had said about Jesse having killed someone.

She listened intently.

"Right after we moved to Wiota I heard talk about the bank robbery," she said.

"What did you hear?"

"That it was somebody named Plockett."

Feeling wretched, I shook my head.

"Early," she asked, "is *he* . . . your uncle?"

Greatly agitated, I could only nod. "I won't believe it was him."

We sat silently for a few minutes as I tried to sort my thoughts. "Lizzy," I said, "I'll wager that railroad office is where the railroad is meaning to go. But to get there, it's got to run right through our farm."

"What's Mr. Mawr got to do with it?"

"Maybe," I suggested, "he's going to keep me from even getting to Cherry Creek."

"Why would he do that?"

"So he can find Jesse on his own. Then he'd try to get Jesse's gold for himself. Why? Because if that gold doesn't get back home, Fuslin—and the railroad—will get our farm."

"Then we have to make sure Mr. Mawr doesn't stop you," she said.

"But Lizzy, if I *do* get through, I might be leading Mawr right to Jesse. Don't want to do that, either. I just wish I knew what he's scheming!" I cried out in frustration.

"Early," she said after a while, "what about . . . about your Jesse killing someone. You think that's true?"

I shook my head. "If I know anyone, it's Jesse. He wouldn't."

She put her hand on my arm. "Early, I do admire your faith in your kin."

I looked at her, trying to tell if she believed me or not. But I did not want to ask. Instead I stared out at the river.

May 20

Though waiting for the ferry frustrated me, our wagons stayed in line on the east bank of the Missouri River. It must have discouraged Mr. Wynkoop, too. Or perhaps he took to heart the word "humbug" when applied to the diggings. After the second day of waiting, he abruptly announced he was going to stay in Council Bluffs and set himself up as the carpenter he was. So he and his family left us.

I only wished Mr. Mawr would leave.

We remained by the riverbank. I didn't want to go back into town. Too crowded, too loud, and too profane. Then there was that railroad office. I kept thinking about what Mr. Bigalow had said when he tried to buy the farm, that the Chicago and North Western Railway might well find a way to *make* us sell our land to them. I had to believe that was Mr. Mawr's job now—to keep me from helping Jesse, or keep Jesse's gold from getting home.

Lizzy, being required to stay with her mother, left me alone to sit by the riverbank for hours, gazing out over the Missouri, which was about a mile across and awful muddy. Even the local people called it "The Big Muddy."

The water was high from upriver spring rains, swirling and snarling with powerful currents and eddies. Amazing to see a river could be so wide or so churning. Truly menacing. All manner of logs, tree branches, lumber, and once a small empty skiff (upside down) flowed with it. I even saw the bloated carcass of a horse float by.

Other times I went to the steamboat jetty, where there were great piles of goods meant to be sold to emigrants going west: bales of dry goods, hundred-pound sacks of sugar and flour, cured meats, coffee, and dried fruits. Cases of lard, molasses, casks of butter, and salted fish. Lumber. Never saw such mounds of stuff. It had been brought on big rear paddle wheelers, mostly from St. Louis city, a city (we were told) much bigger than Council Bluffs, though I could hardly give it credence. I would have liked to see one of the

That's a stern paddle wheeler on the Missouri.
Probably just in from St. Louis.

big steam wheelers, but none came while we were there.

Whenever her mother released Lizzy, we'd wander off and talk—as we did so often—about what we would do once we got to the diggings.

"Jesse and I are going to buy our own farm," I told her.

"I shall build myself a mansion," said Lizzy, "with an elegant ballroom. Once a week all the fine ladies and gentlemen shall come and dance."

"I suspect you'd need to wear something better than calico," I said.

She closed her eyes. "Velvet," she whispered. "Green velvet."

The thought of skinny, big-shoed, freckled-faced Lizzy in velvet made me laugh so, she yanked up a dirt clod and flung it at me.

Mrs. Bunderly was feeling sufficiently better so that she and Lizzy went to the riverside and did some washing. Mr. Bunderly wandered around the waiting wagons offering haircuts and shaves. He found a few paying customers, which cheered him enormously. Upon his return, he proudly held out his palm in which lay two liberty quarter dollars.

"Mr. Early, Miss Eliza," he said, "it is independent commerce that animates this noble nation. It matters not a whit how great or how small the enterprise. Let it be my scissors or a great New England cloth manufactory, each contributes to the wealth of all."

Later, Lizzy said to me, "What do you think of my pa?"

"I like the way his words build up high like church steeples," I said.

"Early," she sighed, "you are a kind and generous person."

When Lizzy was allowed, she and I wandered among the waiting wagons. People were rearranging their goods, or trading with each other. Talking. Arguing. Once we came upon some fiddlers as well as boys playing baseball, the lopsided ball made of stitched leather and stuffed with horsehair, the bat a tree branch.

All during this time, I was intent upon avoiding Mr. Mawr. For the most part, he didn't pay much attention to me. But every now and again, he'd happen to come by. I suppose he was keeping watch on me. Nothing more. Not yet.

May 21

We moved to the head of the line. Our steam-paddle ferry carried twelve wagons each passage and charged *five* dollars for each wagon. If we wished to go on, there was no choice.

We rolled our wagons onto the ferry, set the brakes, and tied the wheels down so they wouldn't move. Then came the oxen. As they were skittish, it took a fair deal of pushing, shoving, and whipping to get them in place. Then we had to calm them, which was my job. Though her mother objected, Lizzy worked with me.

The river's wildness made us uneasy, especially Mrs. Bunderly. She determined to stay inside the wagon and not watch. As for Mr. Bunderly, for once he barely said a word, which meant he too was nervous. Now and again the oxen lowed for the unnaturalness of the crossing.

I was more excited than tense, feeling we were crossing a great boundary, the division between past and future. I suspect Lizzy felt the same, for when she looked at me, she offered a gleeful smile.

As our ferry was getting ready to push away, I saw another in front of us. It was a small, raftlike boat, carrying only two wagons, oxen, and a few people being poled slowly across.

As I watched, that other ferry suddenly tilted to one side.

"Lizzy!" I cried. "Look!"

We stared, horrified, as the people on the raft began yelling and screaming, moving to the opposite side of the ferry while the oxen began to bellow, their desperate cries reaching across the river. It was to no avail: the ferry listed so heavily, so quickly, a pair of yoked oxen lost their footing and tumbled into the river. But they must have been tied to a wagon, for one cascaded into the water, too. It sent up a great billowing splash and was swept immediately away, only to sink in the roiling waters. Behind, the ferry raft righted itself, and nothing more was lost.

But from that ferry came the most dreadful cries of lamentation, appalling to hear. I saw a man restrain a woman from leaping into the waters. We would learn later that a one-year-old child had been sleeping within the wagon that was lost—drowned.

God have mercy!

After the river tragedy, Mrs. Bunderly no longer wished to stay inside our wagon. I, too, was nervous the rest of the way. Lizzy gripped my hand.

We got across and reached the landing place. Once on the far banks, we worked our way through the little town of Omaha, which I was told had been made by the Mormons. Fewer houses than Council Bluffs, mostly log built; a few streets; plus one hotel, and a sea of mud.

We camped in a grove of cottonwood trees, perhaps two miles beyond the terrible river. Mrs. Bunderly sobbed loud prayers of thanks, and I joined in, thinking mostly of that poor, lost babe.

Lizzy sat upon the ground, clutched her knees, and sang softly to herself.

Having seen the tragedy in the river, we were forcibly reminded of the many dangers that lay ahead—dangers of which we had no true knowledge.

That said, we were safely across. After almost a month of travel we had at last entered Nebraska Territory! All we had to do was get across the most of it, and there we'd be, right along Cherry Creek.

With Jesse.

And Mr. Mawr.

CHAPTER FOURTEEN

Into Nebraska

BEYOND OMAHA was a great crowd of wagons. They were just sitting there, as if catching breath for what was going to happen next—crossing what was called the Great American Desert.

The four wagons we had had when we began had been reduced to three. Word was that you didn't dare go across in a train of fewer than twelve. Much too dangerous. You might lose your way, meet hostile Indians, stampeding buffalo, hungry wolves, or catch all manner of sicknesses, suffer wagon breakdowns or dying oxen, or a million other perils you never considered when you began. No wonder emigrants believed in the safety of numbers, with sometimes as many as fifty wagons in a train.

When Mr. Bunderly was about to go off with the men to find a bigger train to join, I heard Mrs. Bunderly say, "Mr. Bunderly, I beg you. Let's go no farther. I'll not survive."

"Cheerful heart," he returned, "you've managed magnificently thus far. Certainly some hazards lurk before us. But with courage and fortitude, we shall find prosperity and excellent health hovering beyond the horizon."

"I am ill, Mr. Bunderly, ill! Words can't cure me."

A little later, I asked Lizzy, "Is your ma doing very poorly?"

"I think so," she answered. "Her fevers come in waves, and she's exhausted. And even more frightened. Early," she said, "I pity her, but her whole world is her ailments. It's too small for me."

I watched and listened as our people, trying to join a bigger train, went around and talked to other emigrants. There was much debate about which route to take, but also about traveling rules—Sabbath travel, liquor, who would be in charge of what: night watch, scouting, hunting, what tasks would women or children do, and the like. Endless rules, debates, and finally agreements.

Even when a train was set, there were debates about

who was going to be captain and who lieutenant. The men all agreed you had to organize military style, this being the only way to deal with the trail dangers. That said, I did see one solitary fellow heading west, pushing nothing but a wheelbarrow into which his provisions were piled. I always wondered what became of him. I cannot believe he survived—but perhaps he did, and struck it rich at that.

In the end we linked up with fifteen wagons—some twenty families, with extra hands like I was—emigrants from Iowa, Missouri, Wisconsin, and Ohio. All told, our train had about ninety-five souls, mostly men, but women and children, too. To be sure, Mr. Mawr was one of the men. He was not going to lose me.

I really did see people head out from Omaha pushing barrows laden with digging tools. I wonder how many made it.

There certainly were all kinds of people crossing the plains.

Our chosen captain was a Mr. Ezekiel Boxler out of
Wisconsin state. He got the post because this was his second trip (he having returned to collect his family), and he
claimed he knew the way. A Mr. Khlor from Missouri was
selected as lieutenant.

After two days of organizing—everything from
nightly guard duty to what kind of card games were
allowed (euchre and cribbage)—it was agreed we'd start
the next morning. Our plan was to take the Platte River
route halfway across the Nebraska Territory, then follow
the south branch of the Platte, which would lead us right

to Cherry Creek. Though somewhat longer than other routes, it was considered safer.

At the last moment, Apollo, Lizzy's pig, disappeared. We searched everywhere, but to no avail. Furious, she believed he had been stolen. I suspected she was right.

"You may not believe me, Mr. Early," she said, "but Apollo was my truest friend. It is hard to think of one's best friend as having been eaten."

"I could take his place," I offered. "I'm not particularly eatable."

She was not amused.

May 23

What can one say about a slow journey across a desert? To begin, I can say only that it made home seem a long way back, and the future that much further. Secondly, it was most amazing how vast the land was. Not always flat but often rolling, sometimes even hilly. In the main, though, it was level, with a horizon always unreachable.

But while you might think such a barren place would have no people, in truth, not a trail day passed without our seeing some settler's home built of wood scraps, an old wagon, or sod, established midway between nowhere and nothing. We also passed many a tumbledown structure that sold liquor, in a world no true spirits could inhabit. Dreadful, filthy places they were; our train always passed them by.

Now and again we saw Indians—the Pawnee people at first, then Sioux, and finally Arapaho, who gazed at us even as we gazed at them, strangers to one another.

Yet the most amazing thing—considering all the open space—was the sight of so many wagons toiling in the same direction as we. Sometimes it seemed as if the entire eastern half of our nation had tipped itself so high, everybody was tumbling down west—an endless parade of big white ants.

This will give you an idea about the great numbers of people crossing the Great American Desert!

At night, when all were camped, you could see fires flaring in a continuous line that marked the trail from wherever you were into the distant darkness that always was there. When I had guard duty—rifle and Mr. Boxler's old bugle at my side, every third night from eight to twelve—the fires were a comfort.

Seeing all those wagons and people, I could only hope that the gold we were seeking was truly abundant. Having heard otherwise, I worried much about the lot of unhappy emigrants with empty pockets, sore bodies, and broken hearts. Had we not already seen some of them? The more I knew of Lizzy, the more certain I was that she would prevail. But the more I understood of Mr. and Mrs. Bunderly, the more certain I became that they'd made a mistake by having come. Too frail, by far.

How often did I console myself with Jesse's words: *I have found gold! Enough to pay our debt.* How much I tried to put my faith in that.

May 24

At a triple blast of Mr. Boxler's bugle we commenced our trek from Omaha in the morning and went five miles across the high prairie. Along the trail, grass grew

With the days dry and the sun hot, the trains kicked up
a world of dust!

abundantly, which meant cattle could graze.

Midday we spied a line of trees far out to the northwest that we hoped marked the Platte River—our main
route west. But first we crossed the Elkhorn River on a
government bridge.

Then, after three more miles, we saw some Pawnee
Indians. Some of them stopped and asked for food. If I
understood matters, they were at war with the Sioux.

It must be said that though Indians were much feared,
and some emigrants recounted tales of stolen horses or

tragic raids, the Indians we saw never committed a hostile act against us.

May 27

It was a few days before we reached the Platte River, which we intended to follow until we reached Cherry Creek. The Platte was wide and shallow, sometimes beautiful, sometimes drab, its muddy waters warm, with many islands big and small.

Nor did we just stay on one side. Since the river had many loops and turns, it created marshlands and quicksands. Here Mr. Boxler's knowledge proved vital, for he led us back and forth over the river so as to avoid such places.

Sometimes the trail was fine though rutted. By the deep ruts, you could see how many countless others had already passed. Other times it was sandy, so wheels sank down. That made it hard for our laboring oxen. All too often there would be but brackish water or sparse prairie grass for our animals to feed on, plus swarms of mosquitoes, who fed on us.

Once, when we were crossing the river, we hauled up on an island only to have high winds blow in, so that our wagons were stuck midstream for two days.

May 30

As we went on, there were dispiriting markers to show the way—by which I mean, the many trailside graves. Mr. Boxler said the trail was the longest cemetery in the world. I could see for myself how many had come, how many went on, and how many stayed behind.

Also left behind were broken wagons, worn boots, discarded goods that had proved too heavy or useless. Once we came upon an abandoned piano.

And bones! Bones of abandoned oxen, of cattle, and once, human bones, all bleached more white than white itself—ghastly ghosts that turned to dust where they lay.

Each object left a story told in silence.

June 2

Though as usual we started at sunup (breakfast: cold bean soup, bread, molasses, and weak coffee), we took a wrong turn and got lost despite our experienced captain. Had to go back. Then we ran short of water and didn't find any until about nine. Only got back to the Platte River in the afternoon. Everybody, humans and beasts, was exhausted.

Indeed, Mrs. Bunderly let it be known that it would not be long before she departed this mortal world.

"Do you think she might really die?" I asked Lizzy.

"My father is always talking and my ma is always dying," was her response. Then she said, "You must think me cruel. They want so little and don't get much.

"Early, you won't believe our migration. From Utica, New York, to Ohio. Then on to Tennessee, Illinois, and lastly to your town in Iowa. Hardly there a month. Now this. Every place we go, we live on the edge of disaster— and always seem to leap just before we truly fall."

I thought of my family, who had *never* moved, and did not want to. To be sure, there was comfort in what I knew. But if I did not know anything beyond home, how could I measure its comfort? As it's said: you can't know the pleasure of an old boot till you walk a new road.

June 3

I saw a gigantic prairie-dog town—as crowded as Council Bluffs. The way those creatures sat up and kept watch on their mounds, then darted about, was comical.

Most nights people gathered around one of the fires and shared stories. Generally they were about their own

I loved watching the prairie dogs. Almost comical the way they sit up, keep watch, and scurry about in their great big towns.

lives, travels, and travails. Sometimes there was a funny story, such as from Mr. Shotcraft of Wisconsin, who (mistakenly) trapped a skunk under his bed.

June 4

This day I saw buffalo, a herd of them, a herd so immense it was impossible to count their numbers—a brown ocean flooding over the prairie, rolling slowly with ponderous magnitude. Our captain, Mr. Boxler, took pains to warn us we must do nothing to rile them, lest they stampede and trample our train to dust.

June 6

We saw antelope, and they were beautiful. Lizzy loved to watch them run. "I'd like to run like that," she mused.

"Get some bloomers," I advised.

June 7

The land we passed over, though mostly flat, had many a sandy bluff, with mostly good water to be found and enough grass for our cattle to graze at the end of a day. I saw some trees—cottonwood, I supposed—but not too many. Wood being scarce, I was regularly sent out to secure buffalo chips—dried buffalo manure—to burn. Though it didn't provide much heat, it fired enough to cook our food.

The collecting of the chips was something the wagon train's children were sent to do. After a day cooped up in the wagons or walking through the dust, they found it a joy to run and screech. But there was always fear that a little one would wander into the tall prairie grass and be lost forever.

Lizzy, released by her mother, and I, by Mr. Bunderly, were very happy to walk free and collect chips, too. Happily, buffalo were many, and chips not difficult find.

One day we came upon a large, sick buffalo. It was quite alone in its suffering. I'd not seen one up close before. It was huge, most likely six feet tall, with shaggy brown fur, a mane, a beard under its chin, and a long tail with a tuft of hair at the end. Its head was truly gigantic, with short, sharp black horns, and it had a hump on its shoulders that suggested great power and strength. One of our train supposed it might weigh a ton.

Mr. Armon shot it dead. The meat was shared, and that, I will admit, was good for a change.

June 8–11

Our endless walking continued. At times I wondered if anyone had ever walked so far! Then I recalled that those who were going to Salt Lake, Oregon, and California were going even farther!

Once, as I was walking, thinking I know not what, Lizzy came along and walked by my side.

She did not speak. Nor did I. Then I heard a great sigh, and sensed her shoulders shaking.

"Lizzy!" I said, turning toward her.

I saw what I had never seen before: tears upon her cheeks.

"What is it?" I cried.

"Oh, Early, will we ever, ever get there?" she sobbed.

"We will," I said, though I too had begun to doubt.

But what choice was there? You either put one foot in front of your other foot, or you would be left behind.

So it was that at last we reached Fort Kearny, a place meant to protect those that passed by. But it was there that Mr. Mawr tried to murder me.

CHAPTER FIFTEEN

Stampede!

June 12, 1859

FORT KEARNY lies on the south side of the Platte River, set back perhaps half a mile, not far from what they called Grand Island. It's an island—Mr. Boxler informed me—fifty miles long!

The fort was built on a slight rise of ground, the only height thereabouts, which gives a long view of the prairie. From it, to the north, we saw a great dark herd of buffalo.

The fort was nothing to speak of: some frame houses, big and small, as well as a few sod houses, all set around a forlorn parade ground. In its center was a flagpole from which hung a wind-tattered flag of thirty-three stars. Two troops of foot soldiers were stationed there.

Fort Kearny was only a little more than ten years old in 1859.
It seemed to be in the middle of nowhere.

We remained at the fort for two days, along with other trains. In some there was considerable sickness: dysentery and cholera. Bad water was blamed. Folks from other trains spoke of contaminated food. At this point, a fair number of people gave up and headed back toward the states. Some of those going on still insisted on calling the returnees "go-backers" or "stampeders," as if they were frightened buffalo.

I stood with Mr. Bunderly as we watched them go.

With a sigh, he said, "Mr. Early, as the poet wrote, 'Fools rush in where angels fear to tread.'" Which he thought we were, fools or angels, he, for once, did not say.

Another reason emigrant trains liked to pause at Fort Kearny was that people were able to purchase some goods from its storehouse. Being the last mail post before Cherry Creek, it was the place where Jesse had sent out one of his letters.

Remembering that, and watching the go-backers, made me think about my family—how far away they were, how much I missed them, even Adam. So I set myself down and wrote a letter:

> To Ma, Pa, Brother Adam:
> I am at Fort Kearny in the Nebraska Territory on my way to the Cherry Creek diggings. For sure I shall bring Jesse and his gold home. Do not fret.
> > Your loving son,
> > Early

Letter in hand, I wandered around the fort trying to find a place where I could post it. Unfortunately, I met Mr. Mawr. Perhaps he had been watching for me.

"A letter, Early," he said. "Who are you writing to?" he demanded.

"A kindly neighbor, back home."

"Not to your uncle Jesse?" he asked.

"He doesn't know I'm coming," I said before I thought what I was revealing. When he made no response other than to look hard at me, I went on to post the letter. As I was to learn, my words to Mr. Mawr were a blunder.

That afternoon, Lizzy appeared with her father's pepperbox pistol.

"Why'd you bring that?"

"Do you know how to use one?"

I shook my head. "I told you, just a rifle."

"What if we find a lot of gold and someone tries to take it from us?" I supposed she was thinking about what I'd told her about Jesse.

I grinned. "Think that might happen?"

"Mr. Early, I intend to find pounds of gold," she said and insisted upon my firing the pistol a few times.

We went out on the prairie, and after choosing a target—the stump of a tree—we commenced, each shooting six times. In the silence of the plains, the noise was thunderous. But in all that banging, I think we managed to hit the tree but once. "Hard to hit anything with a pepperbox," Lizzy said.

"Then what good is it?"

"You can scare people off."

"You don't need that gun to do that."

"Mr. Early," she shouted, "I think I hate you." But she was laughing as she chased me all the way back to the wagons.

June 14

On the second day of our stay at Fort Kearny, Mr. Mawr approached me. "Early!" he barked, for that was his way, reminding me of Adam. "We're in need of buffalo chips. Come with me!"

I was reluctant to do as he ordered. But Mrs. Bunderly, who was reclining in the shade cast by our wagon, called out, "Mr. Early, you must do the bidding of your elders."

I looked about for Lizzy but did not see her.

Mr. Mawr must have guessed my thought, for Lizzy and I were always together.

"I suppose a boy can go without a girl," he said.

Feeling taunted, I pulled myself up, grabbed an old flour sack for the chips, and began to follow, noticing as I did that Mr. Mawr had his pistol on his hip.

We walked along the wagons that made up our train until, to my surprise, Mr. Mawr, who had not spoken to me since we had left Mrs. Bunderly, mounted a horse and headed on to the prairie. I hesitated, but he turned in his saddle.

"Let's go, boy!" he shouted and moved along at a pace which I could follow, his saddle creaking, his Spanish spurs sounding a harsh jangle.

Once, twice, I looked back at the fort, wishing Lizzy was with me, but felt compelled to continue on. Now and again Mr. Mawr glanced back as if to make sure I was following.

I soon realized we were moving ever closer to that herd of buffalo we'd seen. They were grazing, great heads down, moving slowly in our direction. By then we had come so far that the undulating land made it impossible to see either our wagons or the fort. Nor, I realized, could anyone see us. There was nothing else on the prairie save a dead cottonwood tree, which stood like some lost, forlorn creature.

Feeling isolated, I felt a tickle of fright and stopped. "Where are we going?" I called.

Without pausing, Mr. Mawr turned in his saddle and said, "You can start collecting. Plenty of chips here about. I'm going to scout on farther. Maybe shoot a buffalo."

There being nothing out of place in that, I merely nodded, and watched, relieved, as he put heels to his horse and galloped toward the great herd.

I set about my task, throwing the dry chips into the bag, though occasionally I looked up and around to see where Mr. Mawr had gone. He was out of sight.

Meanwhile the buffalo herd continued to drift closer to me, so close that I began to wonder if I—who had no desire to be among the beasts—should not start going back on my own. In any case, my sack was almost full.

Resolved to pick up a few more chips, I bent over, only to hear two sharp pistol reports. I looked up and searched in the direction from which the shots had come. My first thought was that Mr. Mawr was at his hunting.

The buffalo lifted their great heads.

Two more shots rang out.

Something else happened so very quickly, I wasn't sure I was seeing right. In an instant, or so it seemed, the buffalo transformed themselves from a tranquil, grazing herd into a panic-driven mass galloping in my direction, the sound of their feet striking the ground with tremendous thundering.

They had been startled by the shots.

For some few seconds, I stood transfixed, until my

If you took this picture and multiplied it fifty times fifty,
you might get a sense of all those buffalo we saw on the plains.

disbelief gave way to an understanding as to the grave
danger I was in: the mass of beasts was stampeding, and I
was directly in their way. They would not stop or turn
from me—so very insignificant—but trample me to death.

Even as I stood there, horrified, I recalled that solitary
tree some yards away. In less time than it takes to recount,
I dashed toward it frantically, running as fast as I have ever
sped. As I ran, I kept glancing at the beasts that were clos-
ing in on me, their shaggy horned heads low, bellowing
and braying, foam spewing from their mouths and large

nostrils, the beat of their hooves making a calamitous noise that shook the earth itself, even as a cloud of dust and clods filled the air.

At the last moment, I leaped upon the tree and climbed faster than any cat could climb. Some eight feet above the ground, I held to a branch, with little doubt I was clinging to my life.

Like a river on a rampage, the buffalo flowed all about me, an immense moving dark brown mass, churning up clouds of choking dust and deafening sound, thunderous enough to make the dead tree shake as if to come back to trembling life.

I am not sure how long I stayed on that tree, my heart doing its own pounding, my arm muscles aching with my desperate hold. The sheer number of the animals seemed infinite. But it was almost impossible to see because of the dust that whirled and whipped around me.

Their passing may have lasted for as long as twenty minutes. But after charging by and going on, and with no further shots to alarm them, they began to calm themselves. I soon saw them grazing peacefully not half a mile away, as if nothing untoward had occurred.

I dropped to the ground, my legs so weak and wobbly, I could hardly stand. I sat down, back propped against the tree that had saved me, struggling to find breath and wits.

After some minutes, I pulled myself up and began to walk in the direction where I thought the fort was. At one point I stopped and looked about. Where was Mr. Mawr? Though he was nowhere in sight, I had little doubt he had deliberately set the buffalo running with his pistol. That's to say, it was no less than attempted murder.

It made me ill to think it.

I spied the fort. I was still approaching it when I saw Lizzy, red hair fluttering like some signal of distress, running across the plains in my direction.

Seeing me, she halted. "Early!" she yelled. "You all right?"

"Think so," I called and walked on.

She kept running toward me. When we reached each other she stood before me, panting, her face anxious, her green eyes welling with tears. "Mr. Mawr . . . came riding into . . . camp," she gasped. "He said you had been trampled by the buffalo. Killed!"

"Almost was," I said.

"What happened?"

I told her.

"You really think he did that on purpose?" She glanced

toward the fort, as if Mr. Mawr might suddenly appear.

"Remember our talk at Council Bluffs?" I said. "When we were trying to figure out what he was going to do? If he was going to try and keep me from going, or just follow me to Jesse?"

She nodded.

"Yesterday I made the mistake of telling him that Jesse didn't know I was coming out to him. He must have decided he could kill me and go after Jesse's gold himself."

"Mr. Early," she said with sudden anger, the tears now running down her cheeks, "you must promise me never to go anywhere with that man alone. Do you understand? *Never!*"

Though still shaken within, I was touched by her caring. "I promise," I said, grateful that she was there.

Then, to my great surprise, she gave me a hug. "Early," she said with great fierceness, "since the death of Apollo, you are my best and only friend! I won't have you dead!"

I supposed I grinned. "I won't let it happen," I said.

"Do you swear?" she insisted.

"I swear."

"Then we are sweethearts."

"We are?" I said, taken aback.

"Yes!"

"If you say so," I managed, not knowing what to say otherwise, but feeling glad.

Together, we went back to camp.

"Lizzy," I said, "I can't prove what Mr. Mawr was doing. I suppose it's best not to say anything. And since I'm alive, I guess he's going to have to follow me."

She agreed.

When we arrived, other folks who had heard Mr. Mawr proclaim my death congratulated me on my miraculous survival.

Then Mr. Mawr approached, but an angry look from me stopped him at some yards' distance.

We spoke no words but merely glared at one another. For myself I can say no silence ever spoke a more hateful exchange. But then, I suppose mortal enemies require no spoken words.

So it was on that day that I gained both an enemy and a sweetheart.

For one, at least, I was gratified.

CHAPTER SIXTEEN

Going On

June 15, 1859

WE LEFT Fort Kearny early, only to have our wagon break down. One of our rear wheels was off kilter. I had forgotten to tar it properly before we set off. As I watched the rest of the wagon train push on, I thought of what Adam would have said, and I expected no less from Mr. Bunderly. All he said, however, was "Mr. Early, it's been my singular fate to learn that one gains good experience from doleful events. Therefore, good and bad constitute one's education in equal measure. Let us, therefore, rejoice in the increase of our knowledge and hasten to repair the wheel."

In fact, it was Lizzy and I who worked to fix the

wagon, which required much unloading and reloading. As for Mr. Bunderly, he took care of his wife, who was doing poorly that day.

Once done, we hastened on and caught up with the others. As we went, we met a mule-pulled wagon going back toward the states. On its cloth cover was writ large:

PIKE'S PEAK A FRAUD!

During the day a new troubling thought came to me. "What if," I asked Lizzy, "Jesse has already gone back, and we miss him?"

All she said, could say, was "Don't know." But all day, I brooded over such a possibility.

At campfire that night, the men talked about the repeated bad reports about Pike's Peak gold. Anxiety seasoned their voices, some with bravado, others with worry.

Jesse has his gold, I kept telling myself.

June 16

Saw a coyote at a distance. Some of the men went after it. Had more success with a rabbit.

June 17

Very hot.

The men hunted buffalo. They just enjoyed shooting the great beasts. Since the stampede, I wanted nothing to do with the animals.

The rolling prairie had no shrubbery save along the margin of small creeks, where we found a few stunted trees and smaller brush. The river water was shallow and warm.

The trail west left many emigrants and their wagons looking mighty poor. These folks don't even have a matched team to haul them along.

We again met with discouraged folks heading back east. Some of our train cried, "Stampeders!" I sensed their mockery only masked their own nervousness. But the go-backers made me wonder. If all these people had failed to find gold, how much could Jesse have gathered?

June 18

The men killed two buffalo.

Mrs. Bunderly took to remaining within the wagon all day. Mr. Bunderly was grim. Lizzy held the reins. I walked alongside. Almost no talk.

June 19

This Sunday we rested. A good thing, too, for all were exhausted, including the animals.

Awful hot. Coolest place was beneath the wagon. I lay there, and perhaps because it was so still, I gave hard thought to the possibility that when we got to Cherry Creek, I would not find Jesse. What then? I'd be alone. Without money. Far from home. What would I do?

With no answer, I just felt sick.

Lizzy spent more and more time attending her mother.

June 21

Traveled for seven hours and reached a place called Plum Creek. Sometimes the thought came to me that we were doomed to travel forever.

Lizzy jerked some buffalo meat.

She has talked very little.

A picturesque early morning scene of a small family
on the prairie as breakfast is prepared.
Other wagons are already under way on another long day's journey.

June 22

On this day we went twenty miles, or so it was reckoned. We pushed so strenuously that some oxen in our train became lame.

A Mrs. Wulsom in one of the wagons put her day's milk (they had a milk cow with them) in a can and tied it to the backboard. At the end of the day all the jostling had turned the milk to butter!

At campfire, the men debated the merits of the abolition of black slavery. Most were against slavery. Some were vehemently for it. Much talk about the abolitionist John Brown.

June 23

We went eighteen miles and camped near Cottonwood Springs. When we got there, we found some fifty emigrants, who, as we learned of their misfortunes, became objects of our compassion.

They had started going west (from Kansas City) by the Smoky Hill trail. When they realized it was the wrong choice—it being so desolate and scarce of water—they turned north in hopes of reaching the Platte River.

They had begun with horses, mules, and oxen, but when we found them, most were without any. Their teams, deprived of food and water, had perished. They had eaten some of their animals. Wagons had been broken up so that the wood could be used to cook food. Many were sick and desperate. All cursed the day they had ever set forth.

We offered such help as we had.

Later, I saw Lizzy wander off and sit down alone on the prairie. When I went out to her, I discovered she was crying. I had enough good sense not to say anything, but sat by her side in silence as she sobbed.

"Early," she finally said, "one of the ladies on that train became a mother when they were traveling. Her poor babe lived only a few hours and was buried on the margin of a brook. They said they named the place Infant Creek."

"I grieve for it."

"But, Early," she cried with anger, "how could they give the creek a name and not the child?"

I didn't know what to say.

"Mr. Grostig—" Lizzy went on, "he's with that wagon from Missouri—is ailing. So is my mother. What if she dies?"

"You'll manage, Lizzy. You and your father. You'll have to."

"She has suffered too much to die now!"

Unable to find words to comfort her, I gazed out at the empty land. "This is all too hard," she said after a while.

"It is," I said, feeling great pain in my chest.

All of a sudden she clutched my arm and cried, "Early, you must never, ever leave me!"

All I could say was "I won't."

"And if I should die," she went on, gulping back her sobs, "you must not abandon me out here. Because if you did," she said with great fierceness, "I know I'd die anew each day from terrible loneliness."

All we could do was sit together. It was a small thing in a big world—but what else were we to do? I had to acknowledge to myself that when I'd set out to find Jesse, I hadn't known what I was doing, hadn't known (and still didn't) where I was going or what might happen. I felt small, weak, and stupid.

For the first time in my life I wondered: Would I live?

CHAPTER SEVENTEEN

The Long Trail

June 24, 1859

WOKE TO hail big as peas, which later turned to rain.

When the rain finally stopped, some of our train, so discouraged by the unfortunate emigrants we had met the day before, turned back. We were now a train of twelve.

Mrs. Bunderly worsened. Lizzy was grim.

June 25

We rolled on, always looking for water. Reached Fremont Springs, which had some. I supposed the place was named after the man who had first explored this area for the United States.

A curious, grotesque thing occurred. The children found a dead buffalo. The poor beast was so bloated with decay gas, the children took to jumping on it. The gas-filled carcass served them like a spring, bouncing them high. That went on until the bloat burst and a child fell into the beast's putrid innards. Much glee, and disgust.

Fortunately the spring was close.

June 26

We reached the place where the Platte River divided. Follow the trail along the north branch, and you eventually get to Salt Lake, California, or Oregon. The South Platte, however, would lead us to Cherry Creek, and so we turned and camped upon its banks.

I wondered how close we were, how far we had come. There was nothing about the trail to tell us. No markers. No fingerposts. Though surely we were on the trail—the wagon ruts told us so—but we could as well have been lost.

Mrs. Bunderly, faring most poorly, remained in the wagon. Lizzy tended to her all day. When I saw her, she was sad. But sometimes angry.

June 27

Went twenty miles along the riverbank. The water was shallow and warm. Lizzy and I did a calculation and determined that it was *forty-six* days since we had left Wiota! We told that to Mr. Bunderly. He reminded us that Noah was afloat for only forty days and nights.

I told Lizzy what Jesse had claimed, that he could have walked to Cherry Creek on his hands—backward.

"Maybe what your brother Adam said is true," she snapped. "That Jesse's a fool."

"He's smart," I insisted.

She said nothing, which made me sulk over her remark.

There being no wood to burn for our meal, I went with the youngsters to collect buffalo chips. Whenever I left the train, I kept an eye open for Mr. Mawr. I would see him watching me.

How, I worried, would I be able to free myself of him once we got to Cherry Creek? Surely I'd have to get rid of him before I reached Jesse.

Around the fire that night, the men were talking about what it was that made men want gold. All kinds of opinions were offered, but the best was Mr. Bunderly's. He said, "Gold attracts men because its nature is opposite their own. That's to say, no matter how old gold gets, it keeps its value, is forever malleable, and remains bright."

I puzzled that in my head and determined he meant that as a man gets older, he loses his value, does not change, and grows less wise. Did he mean himself? I resolved that would not be me.

June 28

Went twenty-two miles. Passed an Indian trading post at Julesburg.

Now and again we have met Indians—the Pawnee and Sioux. They are different peoples and at war with each other. Sometimes they come and ask for food, or wish to trade for horses or guns. We try to be accommodating about food. We heard some stories how they have returned lost children to emigrant trains. Still, some of our people mock them, but never to their faces. Others are frightened. A few like Mr. Boxler, our train captain, have tried to learn their different languages, insisting we can only gain by their friendship. For the most part we keep our distance—like mutually uneasy strangers.

Indian trading post. Emigrants bought supplies, too.

June 29

During the night, Mrs. Bunderly died.

Mr. Bunderly was consumed by grief. He blamed himself for his wife's demise, bemoaned ever leaving Iowa, chastised himself for not heeding her complaints. Lizzy was full of sorrow, too, but she had to lay her mother out, and insisted she'd do so alone. Then she and her father went out from the trail to dig a grave. Not long after, she came back to me, tearful.

"My father is too stricken to dig," she told me. "I must beg your help."

The two of us dug the grave in hard ground. Lizzy's tears did not soften it. Mr. Bunderly, saying he could not watch, left us.

Lizzy and I went along the trail until we found an abandoned and broken wagon. We took boards from it and made the crudest coffin.

When Mr. Bunderly heard of what we had done, he said, "Dear children, learn from this: the most broken wagon can carry one far."

We buried Mrs. Bunderly the next day. The whole train was in attendance. Mr. Boxler read from the Bible, the twenty-third psalm. Looking about the prairie, I wondered if I would ever see green pastures again.

Lizzy sang. Her voice gave me thoughts of Iowa meadowlarks. My homesickness swelled.

As I grieved, I recalled Reverend Fobbscott's words about a cold coffin in a colder grave. That the day was so hot made no difference.

Mr. Boxler urged that we leave the grave unmarked, lest impoverished emigrants in search of valuables dig it up—as he claimed sometimes happened.

That night we traveled beneath a full moon so as to avoid the heat. The pale yellow light made the prairie seem even more still. We heard coyotes bark, and once an owl gave call. I thought perhaps it was not an owl but Mrs. Bunderly's unhappy spirit trying to follow us.

It made me shiver.

At night, before falling asleep beneath the wagon, I wondered: Is this journey the hardest thing I'll ever do?

I wept some tears. The tears were for not for Mrs. Bunderly, but for myself.

June 30

As we went along, the oxen snorting, the wheels creaking, the harness jangling, I could not help but think of the lonely silence of Mrs. Bunderly's unmarked grave, left ever farther behind, never to be visited again. Even if we tried, we would never be able to find it.

Lizzy must have been thinking the same kinds of things.

"Early," she said, "I think the heaviest burdens we carry are our unhappy memories."

"I shall have only one happy memory of this trip."

"What?"

"You."

"Early," she whispered, her voice broken, "your kindness is as sweet as cool water."

July 1

The hot dryness made our lips chapped, hands cracked, and brows wrinkled. So we "mooned"—which is to say, we traveled all night to avoid the heat. Above, the ever present stars seemed infinite in number. Did they, I wondered, see *us*, and think of us as we thought of them, emigrants traveling through the vast emptiness?

July 2

For much of the night we went along the river. There was little sound, save the heavy breathing of the oxen laboring and the creaking wagons. Once we heard the long, mournful howl of a coyote.

Lizzy walked with me, but I respected her sad silence. She being without her usual joy, I tried yet again to think what I should do when we reached Cherry Creek, but had to admit I didn't know what to expect. If I could not find Jesse, I imagined I would need to find my way back to Iowa. I would miss Lizzy.

Lizzy must have been thinking these same thoughts, for at one point she turned to me and said, "Early, what will become of us?"

I wanted to say something cheerful, but honesty compelled me to say, "I suppose we don't ever know."

July 3

Though it was a Sunday, it was cooler, so we traveled by day—twenty miles.

At one point, Lizzy said to me, "Early, I have a confession to make."

"I'm willing to hear."

"I loved my mother, but I did not admire her."

"Why?"

"My mother used her illness to shield herself from the world. That made her weaker. I am bound and determined to be strong, but I fear I didn't pity her enough. It gnaws on me that I wasn't strong enough to be kind. I can't forgive myself."

"She was hard on you."

She grasped my arm. "Do you really think so? Truly?"

"You did the best a daughter could."

"Early . . ." She didn't finish her sentence, but turned and to my astonishment, kissed me on the cheek, then ran to the wagon and vanished.

I felt my cheek burn—not too unpleasant a sensation.

I used to think Jesse was my best friend. Lizzy . . . Well, she had really become my sweetheart.

July 4

The Glorious Fourth! We traveled twenty miles today.

At campfire, Mr. Griffin and Peter, who had not played for a long while, offered "Yankee Doodle." Being so weary, our hurrahs were halfhearted.

July 5

No travel. Too exhausted. Visited by Indians. They were amazed by Lizzy's red hair. Kept wanting to touch it. One young Indian, who spoke English, called her "Fire Girl." She liked that.

July 6

Light rain. Went just eight miles but saw scrubby pine trees. That gave hope that the desert would soon be behind us.

Mr. Bunderly, still consumed by sadness, talks little. He is like a drum with a broken head.

An Indian camp by a stream.
There are times I would have liked to stay.

July 7

In the afternoon we crossed a stream called Bijou Creek, and in the distance for the first time we saw blue mountains. We stopped and stared, for it was not easy to grasp what we were seeing. Hard to know if they were close or far. Hard to know if *we* were close or far.

July 8

Continued south along the riverside. At the end of the day, we saw Pike's Peak, or at least so Mr. Boxler claimed. Our whole company thrilled. Lizzy said it looked like an immense thundercloud.

But the skies above were a brilliant blue.

July 9

Traveled all day. Mountains always to the west, growing bigger. At first I saw what I believed were small white clouds against those mountains. Then it occurred to me that I might be seeing gold, and my heart was in my eyes. Mr. Boxler disabused me by saying that what I saw was snow. Snow in July! Someone also said that while the mountains were now known as "the Rocky Mountains," they used to be called the "Shining Mountains." I liked that name better. It held more hope. We needed some.

July 10

Passed ruins of Fort St. Vrain. Sunday, nobody wanted to stop. Last of the dried fruit gave out. Coffee almost gone.

The river was pretty. Many little islands. A fair number of trees. I thought they were willow.

Skies so blue, it made my eyes ache.

At campfire the only talk was what people would do with the gold they found. No talk about *how* they would find it.

July 11

Still in Nebraska. Reached Fort Lupton, which, being abandoned for a reason I didn't know, was in complete neglect.

Skies blue. I had never seen such white clouds. Each day, late afternoon, they towered toward the heavens.

Against the far horizon you could see rain falling—like a distant veil.

In the west you can see farther. Having no boundaries, even distance feels different.

July 12

When we camped for the night, we knew that next day we would pass the border that marked the divide between the Nebraska Territory and the Kansas Territory. Growing excitement. We were so close to our great purpose: the gold of Cherry Creek!

Though I'd pined for our travels to be over, I was more nervous than ever. For once we were there, what would I find?

CHAPTER EIGHTEEN

Cherry Creek!

July 13, 1859

AFTER A journey of more than two months and feeling as though we'd walked a million miles through heat and desert, we went twenty miles more and thereby reached the place where the South Platte River met Cherry Creek. We had arrived!

Though there was no town called Cherry Creek, the creek itself was real enough. It got its name from the chokecherries growing along its banks. I tasted them and they were bitter. But the Arapaho Indians—who lived thereabouts—used the juices to preserve their meat.

For most of the year, the twenty-foot-wide stream was a dry streak of reddish sand. When it did flow, it came out

After the long trek to Cherry Creek some folks just rested,
glad not to move for a while.

of the treeless prairie into the South Platte, along whose
banks grew cottonwood trees.

Some explorers from Georgia first "raised color"—
prospector talk for finding gold—a few miles upstream on
the Platte. The gold they got was worth six or seven *cents*.
True, they found more in other places along the river, but
not much. That was enough. The word *gold!* sped back to
the states. To think that so many emigrants came because
of that tiny find!

Stand where creek and river met, look south, and you
could see Pike's Peak looming. Look northwest, and you

could see what they call Long's Peak, a great mountain, too, sharp at the top. Gaze beyond the river straight west some forty miles, and there was nothing *but* mountains: the Rocky Mountains.

They were vast, jagged, monster mountains, cliffs, towers, and peaks reaching up into the sky, sometimes higher than the sky and into the clouds. They had snow that never fully melted, but remained, glistening and glowing white, all year round: a place where summer never came. These mountains stretched clear across the western horizon as if to say "You've come this far, but you'll go no farther!"

In truth, though we had traveled long, hard, and close together—so close we knew the number of buttons in one another's shirt—no sooner did we arrive, foot-sore and weary, than we began to go our separate ways.

I was surprised but glad to see Mr. Mawr's back as he trudged off, never saying a word, going I didn't know where. But since I hardly thought that he'd come so far only to give me up, I knew I needed to watch for any sign of him.

Mr. Bunderly chose to bring our journey to an end on the banks of the South Platte. There, on a dirt path they called Ferry Street, was a small raft ferry that had a rope-and-pulley system to haul people and their wagons to the western side of the river.

Once Mr. Bunderly had halted, he set his barbering tools on a barrel, shaved himself clean pink, then wrote on the wagon canvas:

CHERRY CREEK BARBERING
25¢ SHAVE!

Lizzy and I helped with encouraging words. Then he set out a box to sit on and waited for his first patron to stop by.

Once all was set, he stood before us, hand on heart. "Dear children," he said, "behold Ebenezer T. Bunderly, a living mountain of hopeful enterprise. Let us only hope that my head is not in the clouds."

For my part, I was so eager to learn some news of Jesse, I announced I was going to start right away. When Lizzy said she'd join me, her father requested that we seek a place for the Bunderlys to live.

We started wandering. To either side of Cherry Creek were towns. On the north side was what they called Denver, named after a Kansas territory governor so as to gain his favor—except by the time they did, he was no longer in office. On the south side was Auraria, named after the place in Georgia state where the people who had first found gold came from. As we later learned, the two towns were always feuding—not that it mattered to us.

There were a few dusty streets, eighty feet wide with names such as Blake, Larimer, and McHaa. On them a fair number of pigs, chickens, and dogs ran free.

All told there were, at most, a hundred and fifty houses—for the most part, poorly built log ones with canvas roofs, probably from the wagons in which folks

An early view of Denver (on the right) and Auraria (on the left)

This is Denver after about a year. It really grew fast.

arrived. I'd say a quarter of the houses were not finished and sat abandoned. Some were frame houses, with a few glass windows, roofs, and real doors—but not many. Tents were plentiful. By the creek, some Arapaho Indians were living in their teepees. But in this paltry setting, there actually was a newspaper, *The Rocky Mountain News*.

We were informed that about a thousand people lived in both towns. They were mostly from the states, but Mexicans and Canadians were there, too. They looked much like Council Bluffs people, which is to say young men (salted with a few gray heads), plus a very few women and children. Ragged clothes were the fashion, slouch hats (along with some bowlers and top hats), tattered red wool shirts, and sagging trousers, from which revolvers and bowie knives hung. Boots were worn, but bare feet were not uncommon. And—if beards were ever going to be shaved—which seemed unlikely—Mr. Bunderly was bound to become the richest man in the territory.

To be fair, Lizzy and I looked no less tattered. My garments were threadbare and ill-patched. The hem of Lizzy's long skirt was much singed from campfire embers. Her bonnet was long gone, her red hair woven into one long braid.

As we wandered, I kept glancing back.

"What are you looking for?" asked Lizzy.

"Mawr. Can't believe he just left us. But it'd make sense for him to act like he was going away so he could follow us."

In Auraria, we noted two hotels, one bakery, a printer's shop, two meat markets, a blacksmith, carpenter, tinsmith, and a tailor. There were three dry goods stores. And what stock they had was expensive!

BREAD—Fifteen cents a pound!
SUGAR—Fifty cents a pound!
BUTTER—Seventy-five cents a pounds!

That was more than double—and sometimes triple— the cost back home.

As for saloons, while there were too many to count, there was no church, and there wouldn't be a school until October. For that matter, there was nothing that looked like a city hall, or any kind of government building. Cherry Creek seemed to be about riches and drink.

But what about those heaps of gold that you could scoop up with a shovel such as Jesse had read about in the newspaper? All we had to do was look about and see there was nothing of the kind. But if dirt, dust, and mud were gold, I'd have been twice as rich as King Croesus. The truth was, everyone I saw looked as poor as Job—and just as miserable.

In other words, those first 1858 reports of gold did prove a bust. "Humbug" had been an apt word. But that was only the beginning of the story. In the early spring of 1859, prospectors went into the mountains and *did* find gold. A lot of it. When word got out about these new discoveries, people flocked in from the east. This time they didn't stop at Cherry Creek, but headed straight for the mines.

I asked a man on the street where I might find information about someone.

"A miner?" He spoke loudly, as if not used to speaking. Perhaps he was partly deaf.

"I think so."

"You can look around," he said. "But most folks have gone to the mountains, to the Gregory diggings!" He waved a hand in a westerly direction, taking in the numberless mountains. "Who you looking for?"

"Someone named Jesse Plockett."

The man had been paying scant attention until I said the name. Then he turned, studied me, and glanced away again, as if trying to make up his mind. Shifting back, he pointed and said, "Try Denver House. Blake Street. On the Denver side. Can't miss it. Biggest building in town. If any one knows about Plockett, they will."

Lizzy and I started off. As we went along, Lizzy said, "Early, the way that man reacted when you said Jesse's name—it didn't seem good."

I agreed. "Wish he'd said more."

We walked on, though now and again I paused to look about to see if we were being followed. It didn't appear so. But the man had spoken so loudly that if Mr. Mawr had been close by, he would know exactly where we were going.

CHAPTER NINETEEN

Denver House

WE CROSSED over Cherry Creek on a rough plank bridge and soon discovered the pine-log building we'd been told to look for. DENVER HOUSE was proclaimed over the doorway. It was hardly more than a hundred feet wide, thirty-something deep, and was a single story with a canvas roof.

Off to one side were some corrals for horses. One had a sign over the gate: THE ELEPHANT, that pulled me up short. Was that what was meant by "seeing the elephant"?

Inside, it was hot and dim, with only a little light seeping through glassless windows. A long serving bar ran the full depth of the building. Behind the bar were shelves crowded with bottles of gin, rum, and whisky. Cigars were also being sold. A water barrel of filthy water was there. The stench of tobacco and liquor was thick.

Behind the bar was a big-stomached fellow with a flat, thickly bearded face, large red nose, and ears large enough to hear anything he wanted. Deep-set eyes were streaked yellow, giving them a sickly cast.

On the wall opposite the bar were six small cubicles, set off by canvas curtains. Over them was a sign:

Bedroom 10 cents a night

I suppose they allowed Denver House its claim of being a hotel.

Set about a dirt floor were rickety tables at which some twenty or so men were drinking and playing cards. The only sounds were the shuffling of cards, murmurs of frustration, and swearing. Midst the gambling, someone would call for more drink, which the man behind the bar poured from a bottle into a dirty glass and served. Off to one side was a billiards table. No one was playing.

A few men had their heads down on tables, buried in sleep or stupor. On the tables were coins and feather quills.

A prospector is offering up his gold dust, which will be weighed
in the scales and evaluated. Then he can buy some food.

The quills—as I was to learn—contained gold dust, the
town's principal currency.

When no one paid Lizzy or me the slightest attention,
I approached the man behind the bar.

"Please, sir, can you help me? I've just arrived in
town."

"You have my condolences," the man replied in a loud
voice. "Can I offer you a complimentary glass of Taos
Lightning?"

"What's that?"

"Our special blend of whisky, pepper, tobacco, and
gunpowder."

A look of disgust must have registered on my face.

"Not half bad," he insisted.

"No, thanks," I said in haste.

"Just know," he cautioned, "that from here on in, every drink will cost you a pinch of gold dust." He held up a hand with large fingers. "And my pinch," he said with something that might be considered a smile, "is big."

"Yes, sir."

"Looking for work, then? I can get you a dollar a day plus board. The work is only twelve hours the day."

"What it is, sir, I'm looking for someone from back home."

"You're not the first," he said, as if to say, *You won't be the last.* "Where you from?" he asked. "Who you looking for?"

"Iowa state. A man named Jesse Plockett."

"Jesse Plockett," he repeated and gazed at me with what I took to be more than casual interest, not unlike the man we had spoken to on the street. "What's he to do with you?" he demanded.

"I come from his home—Cass County, Iowa. His family told me to ask about him when I arrived." That part was true. But I lied when I added, "He's sent no word."

"I suppose he wouldn't," said the man. "Mail is slow.

Used to come through Fort Laramie, if it came at all. Got ourselves a post office now. But I'd hardly expect Plockett to tell anyone about where—" The barkeep broke off his words. Instead, he looked around, and bellowed, "This boy—just arrived from civilization—wants to know about Jesse Plockett."

There had been hardly any noise in the place. The barkeep's words made even that cease. Half a dozen of the gamblers turned and considered me with curiosity.

"Who's going to tell him?" the barkeep called.

A man pushed himself up from his chair. "I suppose I can," he said. He flipped his greasy cards on the table. "Nothing left for me here."

The man, who reeked of tobacco, alcohol, and sweat, wore a red flannel shirt and old leather trousers. His skin was grimy and weathered dark, while a thick beard proclaimed him a prime customer for Mr. Bunderly. On his head perched a battered bowler. His boots were broken enough so that you could see his dirty toes. From his much cinched belt hung a bowie blade. His breathing was deep and raspy.

"Sit over there," he ordered in a gruff voice, indicating an empty table in a corner.

"All right, then," the man began when we were all

seated and he had looked us over. "How old are you?"

"Fourteen," I said.

He looked at Lizzy.

"The same," she said.

His eyes narrowed. "You two alone?"

"With my father," said Lizzy. "We just came by wagon train."

"They will keep coming," said the man, as much to himself as to us. "How come you want to know about Jesse Plockett?"

I said, "His family wants news of him."

"Do they?" he said, breathing hard.

"Yes, sir, they do.

The man clasped his hands before him. "My name's Willard," he said, offering no last name. "From Cambridge, Mass. Got here in the late summer of '58. One of the first, sucked in by those reports of easy Pike's Peak pickings. You hear about them?"

Remembering Jesse's newspapers, I nodded.

"Yes, there's gold in the creek," he went on. "River, too, for that matter. Not worth a Boston brag. Work a day and you might get a pinch. Say, twenty-five-cents' worth. Enough to get yourself a drink. So if the work don't kill you, that drink will.

"So I went cross the river, following the creeks up into the mountains. Lots did. Above that settlement, the one they're calling Red Rocks, or Boulder, up at Mud Lake, I met your Plockett fellow. You ever meet him?" Willard asked, his dark eyes fixed on me.

I said, "What's the Jesse you knew look like?"

His description fit Jesse pretty close, so he must have known him.

"You say you came by wagon train?" the man asked. "Working it?"

"Yes, sir."

"Most do. But this Jesse fellow, he *paid* the train he came with to take him."

"He did?" I said.

"So he boasted. Anyway, when I met him, Jesse was panning along Mud Lake. Raising color, too. Not a whole lot, mind, but considerable more than you'd get down here. Worked hard. Harder than most. Stuck with it. Didn't complain. Well, nothing out of the ordinary. Said he had to make money for his people back home. Lots say that. Jesse seemed to mean it.

"Bit by bit he had himself a pile. Some do," he added wistfully, thereby letting us know he hadn't. "Not that I ever saw what he got. But I didn't doubt it.

166

"The past winter was—so they claim—mild. If so, I'd hate to see a hard one. So Jesse worked on. Least till the cold came and the creeks froze. Then he had to quit.

"Came down here to wait the weather out. You couldn't get back to the states. You'd be crazed to cross the winter prairie."

"What happened to him?"

"Stuck here like the rest, counting snowflakes. Guarding what he had. No real bank to keep your dust. No regular law, either. But there *are* thieves. So you're pretty stupid if you talk about what you got."

"Did Jesse do that?"

"He must have. Because one day in February he came in here—"

"This place?"

Willard nodded. "Like a wild man. Had a Sharps rifle with him. Claimed his gold had been stolen. Accused a fellah named Thornberry. From Tennessee, as I recollect. You might guess what happened. Argument. Fight. Jesse shot the man dead."

"Killed him," I echoed dully, my heart sinking.

"As dead as cold rock. Well, folks rose up and grabbed your Jesse. Hauled him away. No jail around here. So they nailed him into a little house down the way.

167

With no regular law courts, the miners organized courts
on their own and dispensed quick justice. When Jesse was
brought to trial, the scene might have looked like this.

"Word got around. People got excited. Well, it was winter. Ever notice how fast justice works when there's nothing else to do? A jury of peers—all fair and square— was gathered. That barkeep was judge."

"What happened?"

"Jesse was found guilty. Sentenced to be hung."

"Hung!" I cried.

"Only, the night before the event, he worked his way out of his jail. Kicked the side out."

"But . . . where did he go?" I said with real dismay.

"In the mountains, I'd guess, somewhere. No one knows for sure. Word has it he went to a place called Gold Hill. Lots of folks there. Good diggings. Anyway, he hasn't been found. If they do, they'll still hang him."

"Did they look for him?"

"No one has the time for that. 'Course, if he shows up again . . ."

"How . . . how can I find him?"

"It was winter when he went. He might not even be alive. If you're looking, try Gold Hill. But I've got a favor to ask: can you buy me a decent dinner? It's been a while."

Lizzy gave him a coin and we began to quit the place. At the door I turned around to nod a good-bye. That was when I saw Mr. Mawr stepping out of one of those little curtained rooms.

No doubt he'd heard it all.

CHAPTER TWENTY

Going After Jesse

AS LIZZY and I stepped away from Denver House, I could not have talked, not even if I wanted to. Hearing that story about Jesse had made me sick of heart, truly frightened. Was *that* the Jesse I knew?

But what Willard said made sense. Jesse saying he was working hard for his family: that was Jesse. His paying his way out to the diggings: I hated to think about how he had managed that. Regarding what had happened at Cherry Creek: it fit the letter he wrote. As for Jesse having killed someone, this was the second time I'd been told as much. And Mr. Mawr had heard it all!

We were moving toward the place where Mr. Bunderly

had set up his shop when I stopped walking. "Lizzy," I cried, "I never saw Jesse harm anyone. Never! It would be so awful . . ." I felt pain raising in my chest. Then I had a memory of him right before he went west: the two of us sitting out in the woods. He'd just shot a pigeon dead. What had he said? "Wish that was old Fuslin." Was *that* the true Jesse?

I don't know how long I had been standing there when Lizzy said, "What are you going to do?"

What I said, barely, was, "Go to Gold Hill."

"Have any idea where it is?"

"Out there," I said, nodding toward those ever-present mountains. At the moment they seemed to be another world, even vaster than the desert I'd just come across.

When Lizzy said nothing, I said, "You see Mawr?"

She nodded.

"For sure he'll be going after Jesse. I got to get to Jesse first. You can stay with your father."

"Early Wittcomb! I would have thought you knew me better. I mean to go with you."

"Truly?"

"Oh, how each day I lament the loss of my pig, who had the gift of true understanding!"

I grinned. "I'm glad you're coming."

"Good," she said, calming down. "Now, are you going to help me find a house?"

It proved impossible to find an empty house, at least not a fully made one. We could have taken an abandoned place, but finishing it would hold us a while, and I was in a hurry.

After much looking, we found a poor but complete cottonwood log house. A woman by the name of Mrs. Rascoe resided there. She had come from Texas the previous fall and was living with her two infant children while her prospector husband was in the mountains. They had built the cabin, chinked it with mud, and then he'd left.

Denver wasn't much when it began. But its streets were sure wide.

He'd been gone for so long without sending word that Mrs. Rascoe wasn't sure where he was. While awaiting his return, she was pleased to rent one half of the house for ten dollars a month.

Like so many other houses, it had but two rooms—or rather, one room divided into two parts by canvas. Another piece of canvas served as window covering. The furniture consisted of a wooden crate and bed. The floor was just dirt.

Mrs. Rascoe was an amiable woman, more than happy to have paying tenants who appeared likely to stay and were willing to talk. "It'll be good to have a woman about," she said to Lizzy. "There aren't many here."

Having located a place to live, we returned to Mr. Bunderly. He had found someone to shave and thereby earned his "first Cherry Creek gold," as he put it. "Miss Eliza, I have established myself," he crowed. "Enterprise triumphs! Progress proceeds! A new day has arrived!"

The oxen pulled our wagon to the log house on a muddy street and there we unloaded. In truth, the space inside the house was hardly bigger than the wagon.

While Mr. Bunderly and Lizzy lodged in the house, I would sleep in the wagon. Since I'd spent so much time sleeping under it, I suppose it was a step up.

That first night in Cherry Creek we ate a dinner cooked on a fire outside the cabin. Mrs. Rascoe offered real bread and antelope stew. While she worked, she told us her tales, emigrant stories not unlike our own. She insisted that great wealth was now being found in the mountains, and she had no doubt her husband would get his full share.

"It must be hard for you, Mrs. Rascoe," said Mr. Bunderly, "not knowing for certain about him."

The woman shrugged. "Well, sir, to be in Cherry Creek is to act as if you know what you're doing, even when you don't. There's hardly any money, less civilization, no law, and too much liquor. You live by your wits or lose them. But if my husband is gone, there's enough men about that I suppose I can find another."

After a moment to absorb this declaration, I asked, "Do you know where Gold Hill is?"

"Up beyond that settlement called Boulder, somewhere. You going prospecting there?"

"The name sounds promising," I said.

She sniffed. "Young man, if we could eat promises, we'd all be fat."

When Mrs. Rascoe retired with her children, Mr. Bunderly, Lizzy, and I remained by the fire.

"Mr. Early," said Mr. Bunderly, "I wish to acknowledge the fact that having come this great distance with good heart and capable hands, you have kept to your word. Moreover, you have proved a fine friend to me, my daughter, and my late wife. Having reached this place of golden imaginings, I herewith release you formally from your pledge. Be free to go where you wish, taking with you the gratitude—but alas, little else—of this reduced family."

"And my gratitude, too," cried a laughing Lizzy, clapping her hands.

"And where," Mr. Bunderly asked me, "do you go from here?"

"That Gold Hill," I replied.

"I wish you well in your search. When do you go?"

"Tomorrow morning," I said.

We continued to sit there until Mr. Bunderly rose up. "Good night. It will be fine sleeping with a true roof overhead again. Lizzy, you'll come along." He started for the house.

"Pa," she said, "when Early goes, I'm going with him."

Mr. Bunderly halted and came about slowly. "My dear Eliza, you are far too young. . . ."

"Pa, Early came with us because we needed help. He needs mine now."

"Help with what?"

"Finding his uncle," she said.

"Ah, yes, the uncle," said Mr. Bunderly. "And does he reside upon that Gold Hill?"

"I think so."

"Dear children . . . and you *are* children." He paused and daubed his eyes. "Miss Eliza, I am sure your mother . . . Alas, she is no longer here, is she?" He cleared his throat. "How long, Mr. Early, do you think your quest to find this uncle will take?"

"Not sure."

"Mr. Early," he said, shaking his head. "If I have learned anything, it's this: though one's prospects become un-wheeled, one must never cease moving forward." He turned back to his daughter. "Miss Eliza, as your father, I would not have you do anything foolish, dangerous, immoral, irresponsible, or rash. I suspect if I told you not to go, you would hear my words with perfect kindness but ignore them. You have a keen intelligence, my dear, you do. I put my faith, love, and trust in that. It's what that woman said, 'Live by your wits or lose them.' I would offer my blessing, but having been so ill-blessed, I have naught to give."

That said, he wandered off into the house.

Lizzy and I stayed behind.

"He means well, Lizzy," I said. "He does."

"I know" was all she said.

I stirred the fire, causing sparks to fly up and disappear, then said, "In the morning I'll ask around, and when I get some idea where to go, we can start."

"I'll be ready." She stood and started to follow her father into the house.

I called after her: "Miss Eliza, you're as good as gold."

"Mr. Early," she said just before she went off, "you ever get to thinking that gold isn't worth the looking for?"

Left alone, I thought of home so many miles away. In my head I composed a letter:

DEAR MA, PA, AND BROTHER ADAM:

I HAVE ARRIVED SAFELY IN CHERRY CREEK. NO SIGHT OF JESSE YET, BUT I HAVE WORD OF HIM. I'LL FIND HIM FOR SURE AND BRING HIM SAFELY HOME.

MY LOVE AND DUTY BOTH,

EARLY

BY CHERRY CREEK

Considering what I'd learned about Jesse, they were

brave words. Not that I ever actually wrote them. Had no pen or ink. Didn't know how to send it. Instead, I pondered Lizzy's words, that maybe the gold wasn't worth looking for.

Then I went on to ask myself: *Did I truly want to find Jesse? And if I did find him, what would I say? What might he say to me?*

All I knew for certain was, I dreaded those words.

CHAPTER TWENTY-ONE

Into the Mountains

July 14, 1859

WHEN I woke next morning, all I could think about was getting to Jesse before Mr. Mawr did. So I went rambling early, asking anyone I met for directions to Gold Hill. A fair number of people knew of it, if only vaguely. Others were more precise. But when I put it all together, I had a sense of where to go.

It appeared Gold Hill was in Nebraska Territory, the Kansas-Nebraska border being not too far north of Cherry Creek. The place even had an official name: Nebraska Mining District Number One. From what people said, gold was being found there in good quantities.

To reach it, we'd first need to go northwest, to that

settlement named Boulder that appeared to sit right below the mountains. Once there, we'd have to trek into the mountains eleven or twelve miles more. All told, Gold Hill was some fifty miles from Cherry Creek—two or three days' travel. But people said trails could be found with ease.

During a breakfast of bread and coffee, I told Lizzy what I'd learned. Pronouncing herself ready, we took our leave.

Mr. Bunderly held my hand in two of his. "Mr. Early," he said, pumping my arm like a well handle, "I wish you much joy in the search for your uncle. Extend my warmest greetings, while ensuring him that any close relation you claim is the instant friend of yours truly. With a full heart, I beg your protection of Miss Eliza, and hope you will encourage her toward more gentle, ladylike ways. By so doing, the spirit of her devoted mother would be intensely gratified."

Lizzy listened to more fatherly advice with patience, promised she'd return in good time, and then gave Mr. Bunderly a fond embrace.

Fortunately, a man with a wild beard appeared to request Mr. Bunderly's barbering service, which allowed us to depart. So it was that we left Mr. Bunderly cheerful and chatty. I carried nothing save what I wore—the rough clothing that had covered my back since Iowa. Same for Lizzy: calico dress and boots. She also carried a flour sack with food Mrs. Rascoe had supplied.

The ferry pulled us across to the western side of the river, to an area they called Highland. Cost twenty-five cents. Lizzy paid. "Father gave me a dollar's worth of coins as a parting gift," she explained.

Upon the river's western bank, we immediately came upon a well-marked trail leading west. The day proving warm, and the sky all but cloudless, we set off.

It was easy at first. We walked with no difficulty, though now and again I'd turn and look back to see if Mr. Mawr was following. I never saw him—or anyone for that matter, behind us or before us. That said, I was aware there was more than one way to get to this Gold Hill.

"What if your Jesse isn't there?" Lizzy asked.

"I suppose I'll keep looking till I find him."

"Early, he might be anywhere."

"I know."

"And if you do find him, what are you going to say to him?"

"I keep thinking about that."

"You don't want to talk about him, do you?"

"No."

"Why?"

I halted. "Lizzy, all these stories about him—they scare me. What if he's not the Jesse I know?"

"Think you really knew him?"

"Lizzy," I cried, "back home, my day didn't start till Jesse got up."

"And now?

I looked away. "He's been gone a long time, but there's a sun in the sky."

We went on. After a few miles, the path we were following became rough, full of boulders that would have made it hard for wagons to pass. Being on foot, we skirted them with ease and kept our pace. Whether we were following Indian or game trails, we didn't know. When we reached trail forks, we always chose the northwesterly direction.

As the day wore on and the heat came down, our talk dwindled, though now and again Lizzy sang. She seemed to know a million songs. I never tired of them.

After traveling so long upon the flat lands, we couldn't be but impressed by the view before us. The mountains, mostly red-brown in color, bore swaths of green that I supposed were trees. And the closer we came to the mountains the bigger they seemed to be, ever more fearsome in their loftiness. They looked to have swallowed half the sky itself. I had little doubt they could swallow us, too.

At about midday we paused by a stream, from which we drank. From her sack, Lizzy got some jerked meat, which was our meal. As we sat there, she also drew out her father's pepperbox pistol from the sack, surprising me the way she often did.

"Why'd you bring that?" I asked.

She shrugged. "Might need it."

"It doesn't shoot right."

"Makes a fearsome noise," she said with a laugh.

All that day we walked, our eyes always on the massive peaks. Here and there, we spotted grazing antelope and deer. Now and again some buffalo. Once we saw an elk. Fields of prairie dogs in their towns were alert to our presence. In the sky were birds aplenty, including red-tailed hawks and magpies. We saw no other people.

We walked until dusk overtook us. By then we'd reached a high point on the plains. Looking east, the land rolled for as far as we could see—to Iowa, I imagined.

Turning west, we looked down into a valley. A few lakes were visible. We also saw the mountains at their fullest, from bottom to lofty tops. They looked to have leaped straight up in one great earth-leaving, colossal jump and were ready to leap higher any moment. It was a vision of strength and might such as I had never beheld before.

Moreover, we could see that beyond these mountains were *more* mountains, and then mountains beyond those, mountains as far as we could see. No end to them!

As night drew down and the dry air chilled, the mountains melted into deep blue shadow. Above, the sky hung full of shifting colors: dark pinks, violet, but mostly reds.

"It's as if the sky is filling with blood," Lizzy whispered.

"Let's hope not," I said.

Untold numbers of stars emerged, and with them a slim moon. Was it, I wondered, the same moon over Iowa? It seemed bigger there. A coyote yapped and was answered from some distance. It wasn't long before I heard Lizzy's steady sleep breathing.

I think it was only then I allowed myself to have this thought: *I hope I don't find Jesse.* For the truth was, the closer I came to him, the farther away I felt.

July 15

We rose at dawn and continued in the same direction we'd

been traveling, down into the valley we'd seen the night before. We observed some places that looked like farms, but no one was working them. Increasingly, the land was wooded with tall pine and spruce. But above the tallest trees, the mountains loomed ever higher.

At some point we must have crossed back into Nebraska Territory. Not that there was any marker. But we continued to follow the trail until we came upon a wide creek of turbulent, white-frothed waters, its clear pools revealing many small fish. Here the air was sweet with the scents of pine and wild rose.

The path we'd been traveling veered about and then went upward, following the bank of the cascading creek. As we went on, we saw more and more tree stumps, suggesting people must have built nearby.

Both creek and path made sharp turns. We followed and came upon a place of quieter waters. More than that: there, at the edge of the water, was a kneeling man.

After two days of seeing no one, it was startling to come upon anyone in such a wilderness. The man's hair hung down to his waist and was only a little longer than his ragged beard. His wool shirt had lost whatever color it might have had, and was as faded as his frayed trousers. He wore an old slouch hat, tipped back, revealing a sun-dark forehead and crinkled eyes. In his hands was a pan into which he was staring. So intent was he that when we drew close and I hailed him, he was startled enough to drop the pan and had to snatch at it. Only then did he turn to us.

"Who the blazes are you?" he demanded angrily. "Sneaking up that way!"

Panning for gold. The fellow up front has boots. The one behind does not. These folks didn't waste time putting up log houses but used tents instead.

"We're heading for Gold Hill, but we're not sure which way to go."

He gazed at us. "Gold Hill?" he said with disgust, turning away. "You and everybody else."

"Have others come this way?"

"Most get there by St. Vrain Creek. Up north. But they're coming. A whole lot."

"Then this trail will take us there?"

He glanced at us only to shake his head. "You'll get lost. Get lost, and you're gone." As if to dismiss us, he dipped his pan into the water and then scraped it along the bottom. Next moment he lifted it up and began to swirl the pan while staring into it. Water and sediment trickled out.

Suddenly he leaned forward, peered deeply into the pan, extended a finger, and poked. He then drew up his hand and held up that one finger. "Gold," he announced without emotion.

"Is it truly?" I cried, quite excited.

"Nothing else."

"Can we see?" asked Lizzy.

The man held out his hand. We bent over. On the tip of his finger was a glittering speck. I looked at the man in bewilderment.

187

"Gold," he repeated, answering my look. He reached behind and picked up a large feather which lay behind him on the creek bank. One end of the feather had been cut off, creating a hollow tube. He tapped his finger over this open end, and then checked to make sure the glittering bit of dust had fallen in. That accomplished, he put the feather aside and resumed his monotonous panning.

"Is *that* the gold that's here?" I asked.

"You saw it, didn't you?"

Lizzy gave me a nudge.

"We really need to get to Gold Hill," I said.

"Find someone to take you," said the man, never ceasing the circular movement of his pan.

"Did a man come by here—going to Gold Hill—yesterday?" I described Mr. Mawr.

"I suppose someone like that came by. Then again, most people look the same to me."

We stood back. "Good luck," Lizzy said as we went around the prospector, careful to avoid his gold-filled feather. It didn't seem to matter that we were going. He continued to rotate his pan.

Continuing along the well-beaten path, we entered a canyon whose rocky walls rose high to either side. The massive stone, dull red in color, was irregular and jagged, impossible to climb. Here and there—as if to defy all sense of nature—we spied patches of growing green, and even a few twisted trees growing out the rock crevasses. Farther up, where there was soil, many more trees grew.

Between the canyon walls was a rough but open space of some quarter-mile wide, through which the creek tumbled. That's where we came upon a cluster of crudely built log cabins, not more than twenty and in great disrepair. Uninhabited, most had no windows. Many doors were

This is Gregory's Gulch, where they really struck it rich in 1859.

just holes. A few of these doors were covered with deer skins.

We looked about in search of someone to speak to and spied a woman by the creek's edge. Near her lay a great pile of dirty clothing, which she was washing.

She was a middle-aged woman, gray hair unkempt, her billowy dress wet. She wore no shoes.

She must have heard us coming, for she leaned back on her heels, hand to her back as if to ease some pain, turned her head, and nodded as much to us as the pile of laundry.

"Miners," she pronounced, "are the filthiest people in the whole world. Don't wash but once a month, and only if in a hurry." Then she said, "You new here?"

"We're going to Gold Hill," said Lizzy

"Lots are," the woman said. "Good diggings. They're finding gold in Left Hand Creek and Gold Run Creek. Where do you come from?"

"Iowa."

"Vermont, myself. Didn't come alone did you?"

"With family," said Lizzy.

I asked, "Is there a trail from here to Gold Hill?"

"Oh, sure. Not that I've been there. The men come here. They don't want me messing with their streams. Not with this," she said, gesturing to her pile.

"We need to get there," I said.

"Hurry on up a bit farther. I thought I saw Dunsha McFadden getting ready to take a supply train up. If you catch him he'll lead you right there."

In haste we left the woman and passed through the small settlement. It was poor, simple, and in ill repair. A stopping, not a staying, place. But beyond the cabins was a line of five mules. A man was with them—dressed like a miner—fixing packs to the beasts' backs.

"Mr. McFadden!" I called.

He looked around.

"Are you going to Gold Hill?"

"Who you be?"

"My name is Early. This is Lizzy. Can we follow along?"

"Suit yourself. Just stay back of the mules. They kick."

Lizzy and I sat on some stones and watched him get the mules in order. "What are you carrying?" I asked.

"Flour. Boots. Picks and shovels. Coffee. Letters."

After about an hour of packing and repacking, Mr. McFadden turned and said, "Let's go."

He went to the head of his line, gave a tug to the head mule's ear, and started on, the mules in step.

We followed.

CHAPTER TWENTY-TWO

Gold Hill

WELL TRODDEN, the trail inclined steeply through an ever-narrowing rocky canyon high above the creek water. In some places you had to lean back to see the sky. Though the water below roared with power and froth, the rocks, trees, and now and again some flowers were in perfect tranquility.

The trail continued upward for some miles, following the twisting creek. Then Mr. McFadden guided his mules across a crest that led us to another creek.

"Sunshine Creek!" he announced.

From there, we followed a high ridge—mostly flat—that brought us into what felt like the very heart of the mountains. We walked on for about five hours, moving up and down, surrounded by endless mountains and steep cliffs. We saw no other people. But flowers—blue, yellow, white, and red—grew in great abundance, sometimes in unexpected places such as high rock crevices. Occasionally the land opened out, revealing fields of flowers as free and fanciful as any crazy quilt. Elsewhere, dark corners were brightened by golden mushrooms, which had poked up on pine-needle beds. Sometimes we came upon patches of

This is Boulder Canyon. You can see it would have been hard to go along the creek. Fortunately, the trail to Gold Hill was higher up.

white snow in dark dells. Splashing creeks appeared, only to disappear. A great horned mountain sheep looked down at us from a precipice. As we passed, a small groundhog-like creature called a marmot whistled rudely. We startled a doe and her two fawns. Once I thought I saw a great elk, its antlers as tangled as branches, who gazed at us with nothing less than disdain.

As we climbed, our breathing became labored. For though we were already high, we kept going higher. I'd feared the mountains would swallow us, and indeed they did. Our way was full of twists, turns, and switchbacks, until I lost all sense of direction. But no matter how far or high we went, there was only more forest, more mountains.

Then, after I'm not sure how much time, Mr. McFadden called, "Gold Hill!" from the head of the mule train. Pausing, he pulled out a battered brass bugle and—like the angel Gabriel—blew a series of blasts to announce his coming.

Lizzy cried, "Look!"

There, in a small valley, below were hundreds of men, prospectors all. They had found gold in what came to be known as Gold Run Creek. That soon extended into Left Hand canyon. Much more gold was found at what was named the Horsfal Mine at the head of Black Cloud

Looks like Gold Hill to me.

Gulch. This was not just panning for gold, though there was plenty of that. Here they dug for the gold-laden ore with pickax and shovel. Once dug out, the rock had to be crushed by hammer, ground by an arastra wheel, or pulverized by stamp mills. The broken stone rock was then washed and searched, much like the panning process, but in long sluice rockers and water troughs.

Still following the mule train, Lizzy and I wandered down the steep trail toward the settlement, watching as Mr. McFadden's bugle calls brought in men—and a few women—from all directions, enough to remind me of a stirred-up nest of ants. We went slowly, not sure what we should do or what we'd find.

We did see many houses and tents, but so randomly

An arastra wheel used for crushing ore.
This one was powered by a horse.

placed it was hard to number them. Many lay in the yet uncut forest. The houses—if you'd call them that—were crude, hastily constructed log cabins, as if no one had time or inclination to do better. Only a few were chinked. Doors and windows were merely holes. Roofs were logs thrown on top, layered with pine boughs. No chimneys were visible, which meant cooking was done outside.

Fortunately, no one paid attention to us. It was the mule train that brought excitement. And whatever value the supplies held, letters were the treasures. As soon as McFadden reached the town center, he retrieved the letters from one of the mule packs and started bawling out names. The men who received letters snatched at them as if they contained life itself. No matter what they had been doing, they went off to read. Those unable to read called upon those who could. We supposed they came from families back in the states and could have been written months ago.

It was fortunate that the community assembled as it did. All attention was on Mr. McFadden. Lizzy and I were able to stand uphill and watch. I scrutinized the men closely.

"Any sign?" she whispered. She meant Jesse.

"No. But I see Mr. Mawr."

"Where?"

"Over there," I said, not wanting to point. "At the far side. By that lean-to. He's watching the crowd, too. Must have been waiting for the supply train to arrive."

"Think he sees Jesse?"

"He isn't moving. Come on," I said, "don't want him to notice us."

"Sometimes I wish I didn't have red hair," murmured Lizzy. We moved up the hill and stepped behind a broken-down cabin. While Lizzy remained completely out of view, I kept poking my head out to watch.

"What's Mawr doing?" she asked.

"He's gone among the crowd. Talking to people."

"See anything of your Jesse?"

I kept surveying the milling crowd, not sure how I was to find Jesse—if he was there—among so many.

"Do you?" Lizzy said impatiently.

"No. Wait!"

"What?"

"Hold on!"

Standing apart from the large crowd was a man. He was dressed like the rest: slouch hat, old shirt and trousers, boots. Bearded. But unlike the other miners, it did not seem as if he had any expectation or hope of getting anything from the train. He simply remained in place, looking on, one hand in a pocket, his posture suggesting resignation. But though I could not be sure, there was something about him that looked familiar.

As the crowd began to break up—the letters distributed—this man turned and began to walk uphill toward a grove of trees. Halfway along he took off his hat and appeared to wipe away perspiration. His hair was golden. I knew then I was seeing Jesse's hair as well as his walk, that ambling, shambling gait I would have known anywhere.

"Jesse!" I managed to whisper.

CHAPTER TWENTY-THREE

Jesse

I GLANCED BACK to Mr. Mawr. He was still in a conversation with a miner, paying no mind—as far as I could tell—to the one I was sure was Jesse.

"Did he see you?" Lizzy asked.

"Don't think so."

I shifted around. Jesse was continuing up the hill. I turned again. Mr. Mawr was still talking with that man.

"Early," cried Lizzy, "tell me what's happening!"

I shifted my look to where I'd last seen Jesse. He was out of sight. I felt panicky.

"Early, please!"

"He's gone. Don't know where. I just know what

direction." I looked back to Mawr. To my great relief he was going off in a different way, caught up in his talk.

"Come on," I said.

"Where?"

"After Jesse."

All but running, my heart pounding, I hastened up the hill, moving in the direction I'd seen Jesse move. Lizzy stayed close. I kept turning around to watch for Mawr. I didn't see him.

After we had gone up the hill some ways, I cut over to where I'd last seen Jesse. What I found was a well-used path. I took it. Lizzy followed.

The path led farther uphill, taking us among the thick trees and countless stumps. Hereabout there were log houses tucked everywhere. Tents, too. Any number of men were attending to their business. No one I saw resembled Jesse.

Out of breath, I halted, and looked around.

"Any idea where he went?" said Lizzy.

"Don't know," I panted. "And don't want to ask anybody. Anyway, he'd be a fool to use his real name."

Being on the only visible path, I chose to keep going. After perhaps a quarter of a mile, the trail narrowed considerably. Log houses were no longer around. I stopped, not sure where to go.

"You certain it was him?" said Lizzy.

"Positive."

"What are you going to do?"

"Don't know. But either we find him, or Mawr will."

Then I noticed what seemed to be a clump of closely packed trees some twenty yards off the path where we stood. When I looked down, I saw the tracings of a faint path that led in its direction.

"Come on," I said.

As silently as we could we moved along the narrow path. When we drew close, I realized that what I'd seen was a small log house set in a grove of trees. Its door was nothing more than a gap.

I halted.

"Jesse?" whispered Lizzy.

I stood there.

"What's the matter?" Lizzy asked.

"I'm scared."

"Of what?"

"Lizzy, I know what happened."

"What do you mean?"

Unable to speak I shook my head, muttered, "Come on," and went forward.

Followed by Lizzy, I stepped inside the tiny house.

With a glance I took in all there was to see: a small, dim room with a dirt floor. No window. In the far corner, a cooking pan, panning tin, flour sack. Nearby lay a Sharps rifle. Down along the right-hand wall, some boards had been laid out. The boards were covered with pine branches. On the branches lay a man.

Soon as we came in, the man bolted up into a sitting position. His hand went right to his rifle, which he leveled at me.

For some moments we stared at one another, he squinting—the light was behind me—as he tried to figure out who I was. I had no doubt who *he* was. Though he looked older and was bearded, filthy, weathered, and worn, it was Jesse.

For a moment, neither of us spoke. I couldn't. And it took him a while to realize it was me. When he did, his face blossomed into that smile of his, that *golly, good morning!* grin that made folks glad he was around. He flung down the rifle and just laughed. Oh, how he laughed, finally sputtering, "Well . . . hel-lo . . . little brother!"

My heart hammering so hard it hurt, I gulped deep and said, "Jesse, why'd you have to rob that bank in Wiota?"

Jesse kind of blinked. His smile faded.

"You . . . you shouldn't have done it," I cried.

Jesse shook his head. "Hey, Early," he said, "that's no way to greet your best friend. Not after so long." He pulled himself to his feet and came forward, hands extended.

I couldn't help it. I held back, my eyes smarting with tears. "You shouldn't have done it!" I shouted. "It was wrong!" I was bursting with anger I didn't know I had had. Trembling, actually. My outburst was strong enough to make him hold back. He looked at me with puzzlement as his right hand combed through his beard and then his hair. He shook his head slightly, then he turned and nodded toward Lizzy. "Who's this?" he said.

"My friend."

His bright smile came back. "Hey, I thought I was your only friend. Is Adam here, too? Sister? Brother Daniel?"

"Just me," I said.

"You? Alone? All 'cross Nebraska?"

I nodded.

"What made you do that?"

In the time since I'd last seen him, I had grown some, but I still had to look up to him. "You," I said.

He stood there, as if unsure what to say or do.

I said, "You . . . stole the money so you could get out

here, right? So you could find enough gold to pay our mortgage debt."

"Hey, Early, remember what they said? That gold was here for easy pickings. Well, I wanted to get some, fast. Before it was all gone. Only, you know what, it wasn't easy. Nothing like they wrote."

"Did you . . . really get enough gold?"

"Didn't you get my letter?"

"Yes."

"Well then, I sure did get enough gold. But it was hard, Early. You can't believe how hard. You think working for Adam is hard? You don't know the word. The hardest work I've ever done. You know what panning is?" he asked.

"Sort of."

"Simplest way of getting gold. Get yourself a pan. Hey, some use a frying pan. Tin is better, because it's light. Find yourself a bend in a fast-moving creek. Make sure it's a sandy spot. Or gravelly. Best be sure no one else is around, either. Scoop up some sand or gravel and water into the pan. Swirl it. Let the sand, gravel, and water trickle out. Slowly. Gold—if there's any—separates out. Because it's heavy it sinks to the bottom. Follow me?"

I just stood there, staring at him, listening.

"You get up at dawn, stand in that freezing cold mountain water till your toes pucker white and ache with chills. All the while you swirl that pan, maybe—what? Ten million, billion times. By the end of the day, when there's no more sun to burn your neck, and you're weary, starving, and got more mosquito bites than hairs on your head, when you're asking yourself who you are, where you are, and what awful sin against almighty God did you do to bring you to such a wretched place, you may have, what?

The artists who drew this put in all kinds of ways of getting at the gold. Panning, sluicing, using long toms, and digging.

Ten cents' worth of gold. Then again, you might have five dollars. Word is that Gregory, on his first strike, made six *hundred*! But that was placer gold. Digging.

"Early, let me tell you, you eat miserable food—whatever grub you might have at hand—sleep on the hard ground, and come the dawn, guess what you do?"

"Can't," I said, feeling miserable.

"You start all over again. Is it hard? Oh, it is. Will it make you rich? Probably not. But then again . . ." he added almost wistfully, "for some . . . But, Early, I *did* get enough. Enough to pay that debt. To make that farm ours. Or at least Adam's. To pay back Fuslin for his . . . loan. But . . ." Jesse's voice trailed away to nothing.

After a moment of silence, he said, "Someone stole it. I guess I wrote you that, too, didn't I?"

I nodded.

He hesitated. "You . . . you hear the rest?"

"You shot the thief. First you robbed the bank, then you killed a man. For gold."

"Early," he said with sudden anger, "it's not like back home. Nothing like. No law out here. None."

"They put you in prison."

"Thieves put me in prison!" he cried. "Considered great sport to hold a hanging, especially in the winter when there's nothing else to do. I wasn't going to wait for that. No, sir! Got away and came up here," he said. "No one really cares who you are up here. Or what you did. I go by the name of Adam. Don't that make you laugh?" He broke into his smile. "And guess what?"

"What?"

"I've made enough gold—again, Early—to clear the debt. The folks—even old Adam—don't have to worry. I can give it to you right now."

"But, Jesse," I cried, my heart feeling as if it were breaking, "why did you have to do what's wrong!"

"Early, I'd have thought it would make you glad I got enough gold. Worked hard for it. Twice! Ain't that worth something more than you snapping at me? You should be thanking me. The whole family should be thanking me. Adam, most of all." He had stopped smiling.

"Jesse," I said, tears coming down my cheeks, "I came here to help you. To tell you there's a man who has stalked you all the way from Iowa. Here, now, in Gold Hill. Judge Fuslin sent him. If he gets to you he'll take you back—or kill you."

He glared at me. "How did he know I was here?"

"He . . . he followed me," I said, full of agony.

Jesse looked at me, and in that look I saw such

hateful fury—something I'd never seen before in him. It tore my insides as if it were a knife.

He turned to Lizzy, then back to me again. "Early, that true? You *brought* him here?"

"Honest."

"You always so stupid honest?" he spat out.

"Jesse . . ."

"Hey, Early, we ain't little kids no more. Start living what's real!" His scorn hurt me so.

"Jesse," I cried, "Fuslin's man tried to kill me. I think he wants your gold for himself."

Jesse gazed at me, then turned abruptly and went to the far corner of his little house, knelt, and dug at the dirt floor like a dog digging up a bone. The earth gave way with ease. In moments, he had worked out a hole, reached into it, and pulled up a wooden box maybe six inches square. He hefted it and then held it out to me.

"Here," he said, standing up. "It's everything I got. Take it and get on back home. It should be enough."

"What is it?"

"What do you think? Gold! Got it fair, Early!" He was shouting at me. "All honest work. No stealing. No killing."

When I held back, he spoke softer, almost pleading, "Look here, little brother, I did it for you. And for my sister and your Pa. Not for Adam, though I guess he'll keep the farm with it, won't he? You just make sure and tell him I've taken on his name. That'll make him wince," he said with a grin.

When I still didn't move, Lizzy took the box. From the way she held it, I could see it was heavy. She knelt and put it in her sack.

"What are you going to do?" I asked Jesse.

"If what you say is true, if you brought this man out here to—"

"I didn't mean . . . He's still down below," I said.

"Then don't you think I'd best get moving? Somewhere. Maybe to the Gregory diggings. Don't matter. Out here, people don't ask much. Unless," he added, his face close to mine, "it's their little brother."

"Do you want me to go with you?"

"I suspect you'd be too preachy on me," said Jesse. "All that honesty." He was hastily gathering up his pot and pan, putting them into the flour sack. Took up his rifle, too. "Anyway I need you to take that gold back. They'll love you for that."

I stood there, angry, wretched, bewildered, not knowing what to say.

He pushed past me to the door. "Look here, Early. I'm

sorry for what I did. Truly am. Maybe it'll all work out. And I'm glad you came. We still best of friends, little brother?" He held out a hand. "Yes? No? You going to forgive me? Only got a minute."

I stood there for a moment, then leaped forward and hugged him. "I just wanted to help you!" I cried.

He dropped his stuff and hugged me back. "Hey, Little Brother, you saved me from a hanging, here or home. You can't be more loving than that, can you?" He broke away and turned to Lizzy. "He's the good one," he said. "The best." Then he gathered up his sack and rifle, turned, and rushed out.

I ran to the door. "Jesse! Will you ever come back?" I called. "Jesse!" But he was running so he didn't answer.

Lizzy was at my side. We watched Jesse rip up the path, saw him make a turn heading higher, then disappear among the trees. Automatically we both looked the other way, and that's when we saw Mr. Mawr and three other men coming toward the cabin. They had rifles in their hands.

CHAPTER TWENTY-FOUR

Escape!

"LIZZY," I cried. "It's Mawr."

She ran back into Jesse's cabin and the next moment returned with the pepperbox pistol in both hands. Red hair streaming, green eyes fierce, she lifted that pistol, aimed high in the direction of the approaching men, and pulled the trigger six times.

Six explosions, one after the other. The loudest sounds I ever did hear.

The men, taken by surprise, came to a quick halt, turned, gawped, and fled back down the hill.

Lizzy snapped back her hair and said, "Mr. Early, I can't hit anything with this stupid thing." That said, she flung the pistol among the trees.

Oh, my Lizzy was a beauty then!

I dove back into the cabin, grabbed up the sack with the gold, and bolted out. "Come on!" I yelled.

We scrambled off the path, into the woods, running some twenty yards or so before squatting down behind some trees.

I peeked out. Mr. Mawr and the other men were creeping back, but very carefully. They were skulking behind trees, supposing that whoever shot at them was still in Jesse's place. I don't think they ever saw us.

"Come on!" I hissed to Lizzy.

We backed off quiet and fast as possible, moving downhill. When we got to the edge of Gold Hill, we skirted around it, then went around the valley. Anytime we thought we'd run into people, we went another way, until we came around to the trail by which we had come from Boulder.

And let me tell you, that gold was heavy.

Constantly looking behind, we made our way until it was too dark to go any farther.

In all that time we hardly talked. It was only when night had truly come—as if, perhaps, Lizzy didn't want to see my face—that she asked, "Early, did you always know that Jesse robbed the bank?"

"I thought it, but didn't want to."

"Starting when?"

"Back home."

"Why?"

"The night the bank was robbed, I knew he'd gone out of the house. He told me he was on the porch all night. But someone saw him in town. I'll give him this: he never actually said he didn't do it. Then he paid his way out here. There was only one way he could have gotten money to do that. I just thought if I got to him, there'd be some way to help him."

"What do you think will happen to him now?"

I thought for a bit, started to speak, changed my mind, and said only, "I don't know."

She gazed at me but asked no more.

In the morning, by first light, we opened the bag, took out that box, and looked inside. It was what Jesse had said it was: gold. Even a few nuggets. It looked much like what you think it would look like: beautiful, glittering stuff, the stuff you dream about.

What a shame the dreams it brought were so hard.

CHAPTER TWENTY-FIVE

The Rest of My Life

IT'S NOT really worth the telling about our getting back to Cherry Creek. We got there same as we came, walking. Once we returned to that settlement, the one called Boulder, we kept heading east, traveling mostly by night but always carrying that heavy load. Took us two days to get to Gold Hill. Took us five to get back to Cherry Creek.

We went right to Mr. Bunderly and told him what had happened. Showed him the gold.

"Dear children," he said, "I don't know whether to be aghast or amazed!" But with a sigh, he allowed himself to touch it gingerly.

"Mr. Early," said Mr. Bunderly, "what do you do now?"

"I need to go back to Iowa," I said. "Bring my folks the gold."

Lizzy said, "I keep telling him to take the new stagecoach. It costs. But he's got enough. And it's faster. Safer."

"Mr. Early," said Mr. Bunderly, "I have learned in good times and bad that Miss Eliza is wise beyond words."

The stagecoach going back East was much faster than coming west!

"I suspect you're right," I said.

So that's what I did. Since we had first started out from Iowa so long ago, a stagecoach company—the Leavenworth and Pike's Peak Express Company—had begun service from Cherry Creek to the Kansas border. I took a brand-new, red-and-yellow Concord stage east, squeezing into the fifteen-inch-wide spot my ticket bought me. How long had it taken us to come out west? Months! How long did it take me to go back home? Nineteen days to the Missouri River. Truly amazing. Why, I slept in post house beds (three to a bed) each night.

But first there had to be my good-byes to Lizzy. I promised her I'd come back.

"Mr. Early," she said, with that toss of her hair, "I will wait for you for exactly one year."

"I'll come," I said. "I really will."

"Two years," she amended.

So it was that I returned to Iowa and Wiota, keeping Jesse's box of gold real close. As I looked so young, no one could have guessed what a fortune I was carrying. In the end, I just walked into our house and set the gold on the table.

First, they were amazed. Then, glad to see me. But the questions had to come.

"How did you get it?" demanded Adam.

"It was just how Jesse said: got it with an ax, hatchet, and a frying pan! Easy."

"But where is Jesse?" Ma asked.

"I never found him," I said.

I stayed in Iowa only a short time. Truth is, I no longer felt as if I belonged there. It seemed so much the same, whereas I knew I had changed. But most of all, I was anxious to get back to Cherry Creek. I kept thinking of the mountains, the huge blue skies, the flowers—and most of all, Lizzy. My fire girl.

I went to Judge Fuslin's bank and had the satisfaction of giving him three hundred dollars worth of gold. Said I got it out of the Cherry Creek mines, which was true enough. I insisted on a receipt.

Once I had attended to that, I told my parents and brother that I was going back to Cherry Creek. "The farm is safe and Adam will have it," I told them. "I've got to find my own way."

They argued, of course—my ma, mostly—but I had made up my mind.

So once more I set out for the Pike's Peak diggings. This time it wasn't gold I was seeking, nor Jesse. It was Lizzy I wanted to see, and while she was many things, she was no elephant. I knew she'd be there and that she would sing her sweet songs, call me Mr. Early when she was mad, toss her red hair, make her green eyes shine, and do things that would surprise me enough to keep me glad to be alive.

I guess what I wanted—needed—most of all was to be alive.

I never saw Mr. Mawr again.

Or Jesse.

But I did think about Jesse, often. When I did, I always recalled Lizzy's question: *What do you think will happen to him?* Truth is, I had an answer even then, but that was one of the few times I didn't tell her what was in my mind. I couldn't. Not then. Not ever. I suppose in every heart there's a secret sadness. True for me. I had decided it was the minister's words that said it best:

Gold looks like a god's eye, bright, bold, and beautiful. It's smooth and soft, the way a god's touch should feel. You can bend it, shape it, and darn near chew it. It won't change on you. It won't rust. Get enough gold in your hands, and you can buy yourself a palace.

But, gold can make a person crazy. Because if you get gold seeping into your heart and mind, if you let it

take over your soul, it will turn you into a hard devil.
Then the only thing your gold can buy you then is a cold
coffin in a colder grave.

Jesse, I keep you in my mind, alive and shining. The way you used to be.

To Cherry Creek We'll Go

Then, Ho! Boys, ho! To Cherry Creek we'll go.
There is plenty of gold out west we're told
In the new El Dorado.

We expect hard times, we expect hard fare,
And sometimes sleep in the open air;
We'll lie on the ground and sleep very sound,
Except when the coyotes bark all around.

The gold is there most anywhere,
You can take it out rich with an iron cro-bar;
And when it's thick, with a shovel and pick.
You can take it out in lumps as big as a brick.

Now, ladies, don't you be alarmed,
For we're the boys that are well armed.
Don't you fear nor shed a tear,
But patiently wait about one year.

Then, Ho! Boys, ho! To Cherry Creek we'll go.
There is plenty of gold out west, we're told
In the new El Dorado.

GLOSSARY

ARASTRA WHEEL: A large stone wheel, usually turned by a donkey, used for crushing gold laden ore, so that the gold could be extracted.

BUFFALO CHIPS: Dried buffalo manure used as burnable fuel when wood was not available.

CALICO: A kind of cheap cotton fabric with figured patterns. Originally from Calicut, India, from which it derives its name.

CLAY, HENRY (1777–1852): Highly influential and controversial Whig statesman and member of Congress.

COLT REVOLVER: Weapon invented in 1836 by Sam Colt that was capable of firing five or six bullets without reloading, by use of a revolving cylinder. In the nineteenth century, Colt guns were the best known in the world.

EL DORADO: Refers to a legendary American tribal leader who covered himself in gold. By extension it came to refer to a fabled city of gold. There are many cities and towns with that name.

EMIGRANT: Someone who travels from one part of a country to another.

FINGERPOST: A directional sign which, at one end, has a pointing finger.

FREMONT, JOHN CHARLES (1813–1890): Teacher, explorer, soldier, politician. Early traveler in the Rocky Mountains and California. Instrumental in the establishment of California's independence (from Mexico) movement, and Republican candidate for president of the United States in 1856.

GIG: A light, open, two-wheeled, one-horse carriage.

GOLD HILL: A small mountain town in current-day Colorado. In 1859, it was part of the Nebraska Territory. Large quantities of gold were found there.

IMMIGRANT: Someone who travels from one country to another.

JERKED MEAT: Meat preserved by cutting it in long slices and drying it.

JOHN BROWN (1800–1859): Born in Connecticut, Brown became a militant abolitionist. His anti-slavery efforts in Kansas made him nationally known, even as he was honored and hated.

THE KANSAS TERRITORY: Originally part of the Louisiana

Purchase 1803, known as the Great American Desert, and designated permanent Native American country. The territory was established in 1854, and quickly became a battleground for anti- and pro-slavery politics.

THE NEBRASKA TERRITORY: Part of the Louisiana Purchase, whose Platte River became the central trail west to Oregon, California, Salt Lake, and Colorado. The territory, established in 1854, originally reached the Canadian border.

PANIC: The old term for a severe economic crisis. Today we speak of an economic recession or depression.

PIKE'S PEAK GUIDES: There were numbers of these written. A great many reflected no true knowledge of Pike's Peak, how to get there, or prospecting for gold.

PEPPERBOX REVOLVER: A multi-shot handheld pistol. It was invented in the 1830s and meant primarily for self-defense at close quarters, but was famously hard to aim and often erratic in its firing. With the emergence of the much better Colt revolver, it went out of use. It got its name from the black gunpowder it used.

PIKE'S PEAK: Located near Colorado Springs, Colorado, it was named after the first American who recorded it (1806), a military officer named Zebulon Pike. Pike's Peak is the thirty-first highest peak out of fifty-four Colorado peaks at 14,110 feet above sea level.

ROCK FEVER: Also known as undulant fever, or by its medical name, brucellosis. Causes irregular fevers, pain, weakness, sweating, and depression.

SEEING THE ELEPHANT: A popular phrase meaning to go west, to look for gold. It also could mean going west, *not* finding gold, and coming back the wiser.

SINKHOLE: A depression or hole in the land made by water or other geological shifting. They vary in size and depth and may form suddenly or gradually.

SOD HOUSE: A house built of bricklike squares of earth and grass, or sod.

WHIG PARTY: A political party which came into existence in the mid-1830s in opposition to the Andrew Jackson Democrats and the politics they represented. Whigs were associated with manufacturing, commercial, and financial interests. In the mid-1850s, they were succeeded by the Republican party.

AUTHOR'S NOTE

There have been many gold rushes in American history: in Georgia, California, Idaho, North Dakota, and Alaska, to name a few. These "rushes" caused many thousands to migrate and helped establish the United States as we know it today.

Part of the legacy of these migrations is countless letters and diaries, which constitute the source for many a history. The accounts are by turns inspiring, sad, exhausting, and astonishing. It is these personal accounts which, in the main, I have used to tell the fictional story of Early Wittcomb.

Colorado's gold rush had a number of phases. The first, which began it all, came about when traces of gold were found in and about the South Platte River—present-day Denver. "Pike's Peak or Bust," was the rallying cry for the 1858–59 rush to Cherry Creek, then part of the Kansas Territory. It proved very disappointing, and many who went

225

returned to their eastern homes. But some of those who stayed trekked into the Rocky Mountains, and there, great quantities of gold were found. The gold rush resumed, quickly drawing in more than sixty thousand prospectors and their families. In 1876, Colorado became a state, assembled from parts of Kansas, Nebraska, New Mexico, and Utah territories. The native peoples, the Utes and Arapaho, were driven out or forced onto reservations.

Over the years, more than a billion dollars in gold was found, so much that a mint had to be established in Denver. When the state capitol building was erected in the 1890s, its dome was covered with 24-karat gold to honor the state's original source of wealth. Gold is still being mined in Colorado today.

Although the mile-high city of Denver looks quite different today than it did in 1859, you can still see traces of that gold rush city. Cherry Creek still flows through Denver. A fair number of the downtown streets are just where they were laid out in the nineteenth century, many with their original names. The unmarked spot where gold was first found is near a small bridge over the much-reduced South Platte River. Gold Hill was and is a real place, albeit a tiny mountain village forty miles from Denver. And fittingly, Denver's professional basketball team is called the Nuggets.

A final word: Having done all this research about gold, I decided to try a little gold panning myself. I went high into the mountain wilderness and searched for a creek. With prospector's pan in hand, I spent a few hours panning. Then I brought what I had found to a Denver jeweler. He said, "Looks like you got yourself a few flakes of gold."

Sculpture of a miner in Denver

ACKNOWLEDGMENTS

Thanks to the Colorado Historical Society and its director, Rebecca Lintz, and James K. Jeffrey of the Western History Department, Denver Public Library. For readings for historical accuracy, I need to thank Kathy Yuran and Carol A. Edwards. Particular appreciation goes to Emily Schultz of Hyperion Books for Children for her exhaustive and exhausting work in support of the *I Witness* books.

BIBLIOGRAPHY

Bennett, Robert, comp. *We'll All Go Home in the Spring. Personal Accounts and Adventures as Told by the Pioneers of the West.* Walla Walla, WA: Pioneer Press, 1984.

Brown, Robert L. *The Great Pikes Peak Gold Rush.* Caldwell, ID: Caxton Printers, 1985.

Eggenhofer, Nick. *Wagons, Mules and Men. How the Frontier Moved West.* New York: Hastings House, 1961.

Freedman, Russell. *Children of the Wild West.* New York: Clarion, 1983.

Helm, Mike, comp. *Conversations with Pioneer Women.* Eugene, OR: Rainy Day Press, 1981.

Klinglesmith, Dan, and Patrick Soran. *Colorado: A History in Photographs.* Denver: Altitude Publishing, 1998.

Marcy, Randolph B. *The Prairie Traveler*. New York: Berkley Publishing, n.d. Reprint of 1859 guidebook.

Sanford, Mollie Dorsey. *Mollie: The Journal of Mollie Dorsey Sanford in Nebraska and Colorado Territories 1857–1866*. Lincoln, NE: University of Nebraska Press, 1959.

————. *My Folks Came in a Covered Wagon: A Treasury of Pioneer Stories*. Topeka, KS: Capper Press, 1956.

Voynick, Stephen M. *Colorado Gold*. Missoula: Mountain Press, 1992.

West, Elliot. *Growing Up with the Country: Childhood on the Far Western Frontier*. Albuquerque: University of New Mexico Press, 1989.

Young, Bob and Jan. Pikes Peak or Bust. *The Story of the Colorado Settlement*. New York: Messner, 1970.

Zomonski, Stanley W. and Teddy Keller. *The Fifty-Niners: A Denver Diary*. Denver: Sage Books, 1961.

ILLUSTRATION CREDITS

Image on page 2 courtesy of the University of Iowa

Image on page 3 from *The Hub*, Vol. 24, March 1883

Map on page 13 and images on pages 118 and 124 courtesy of the Nebraska State Historical Society

Image on page 21 from *Pike's Peak Gold* by John M. Eatwell and David K. Clint III, Las Vegas, Nevada: Effective Graphics, 2000.

Image on page 35 courtesy of the Union Pacific Museum

Image on page 46 based on a blueprint by Ivan Collins, courtesy of the Oregon Historical Society

Courtesy of the Denver Public Library:
Image on page 53 from *Harper's New Monthly Magazine*, Vol. 49, issue 296
Image on page 105 from *Harper's Weekly*, December 23, 1871
Paintings on pages 88, 96, 107, and 109 by William Henry Jackson
Images on pages 152 and 172 from *Frank Leslie's Illustrated Newspaper*, August 20, 1859
Image on page 189 from *Frank Leslie's Illustrated Newspaper*, December 15, 1860
Images on page 156, 162, 193, and 195 from the DPL Western History Collection

Courtesy of the Colorado Historical Society:
Images on page 64 and 131 from *Harper's Weekly*, August 13, 1859
Image on page 104 from *Frank Leslie's Illustrated Newspaper*, May 21, 1859
Image on page 168 from *Frank Leslie's Illustrated Newspaper*, November 27, 1886

Images on pages 74, 81, 113, 133, 141, and 147 courtesy of the New York Public Library

Map on page 79 from *Precious Dust: The American Gold Rush Era* by Paula Mitchell Marks, New York: William Morrow, 1994

Images on pages 83, 91, 196, and 205 from *Beyond the Mississippi* by Albert E. Richardson, New York: Bliss & Co., 1867

Image on page 155 from the pamphlet titled "Denver City and Auraria, the Commercial Emporium of the Pike's Peak Gold Regions in 1859," by Theodore Schrader, lithographer. St. Louis: 1859

Image on page 186 © Corbis

Image on page 215 from *Harper's Weekly*, January 27, 1866

Photograph of sculpture on page 227 courtesy of Avi